Simply Pool

Simply Pool

A Short Course in Better Billiards

Joe Hardesty

Burford Books

Copyright © 1998 by Joe Hardesty

All Rights Reserved. No part of this book may be reproduced in any manner without the express written consent of the publisher, except in cases of brief excerpts in critical reviews and articles. All inquiries should be addressed to: Burford Books, Inc., P.O. Box 388, Short Hills, NJ 07078.

Designed by Tony Meisel

Printed in the United States of America

10 9 8

Library of Congress Cataloging-in-Publication Data

Hardesty, Joe.
    Simply pool: a short course in better billiards / Joe Hardesty
        p   cm.
    Includes Index
    ISBN 1-58080-061-0 (pbk.)
    1. Pool (Game)   I. Title
GV891.H34 1998
794,7'3—dc21   98-18869
                                          CIP

CONTENTS_____

INTRODUCTION

Why another instruction book on billiards? There are already books on the subject by such authors as Willie Mosconi, George Fels, Steve Mizerak, and Ray Martin, all endowed with a high degree of natural ability—so much talent, in fact, that they never had to learn how to shoot pool, they had only to learn the subtle nuances of advanced play.

Consider Willie Mosconi, who at the age of six was running the table, at seven was putting on exhibitions, and won the first tournament he ever entered. He never had to learn to play the way you and I did. Consequently, books by Mosconi and other top players tend to explain the game instead of teach the game.

This book will add a unique dimension to the subject. The presentation is from the perspective of an average player who learned the game from the ground up. The goal of *Simply Pool* is to offer a resource upon which to build a solid foundation in pocket billiards. Beyond just explaining the game, this book provides a fundamental understanding of how a beginner with average ability can play the complete game.

There is no right way and no wrong way to do anything in the game of pool. Nor is there a best or worst piece of equipment. The techniques that work for you are the right ones. The equipment you prefer is the best.

Recommendations I make or products I mention in this book are intended to offer you a point of departure. Because pool is a game of infinite variations, virtually nothing works the same for everyone. Consequently, it is vitally important to take new equipment, ideas, theories, and techniques to the table and determine if and how they work for you. Keep an open mind to all new ideas, but trust none until you prove them to yourself.

Most other billiard instruction books treat every aspect of the game in laborious detail, regardless of how rarely encountered, thus obscuring the truly important topics. This book will take a different approach: I'll provide the basic theories you need to develop a complete game. If it seems that some areas of this book are too brief, it's because I feel the topic is best digested through actual practice; little would be accomplished by verbal overkill.

1 THE BASICS _____

ABOUT POOL

Let me first clarify the differences among billiards, pocket billiards, and pool. Billiards uses three balls and is played on a table similar to a pool table, but without pockets. Pocket billiards is the official name of the game played on a billiard table containing pockets. It is played with 15 colored balls plus the solid-white cue ball. The term *pool* was originally slang for *pocket billiards,* because that game was played in pool halls—so named because they acted as betting pools. Today, billiards and pocket billiards are distinctly different games, but pocket billiards and pool are one and the same.

What is the objective of pool? Most players would say that it's to pocket balls. This is true only at the most elementary level of the game. The real goal of pool is cue-ball control. If you have good cue-ball control, you can pocket balls, play position, and play safeties—and hence excel at all aspects of the game.

The player who's an excellent shotmaker but does not practice good cue-ball control will likely remain in the lower rankings. He's like a drag racer who can drive incredibly fast but has not learned to control the vehicle at all speeds. The results are obvious.

It isn't possible to learn pool incrementally—you cannot learn one task completely and then progress to the next. Instead, you must learn the complete game. Then each advancement you make will improve all areas of your game.

All improvements in your game will come from actual practice and play. The feeling of the cue stick hitting the cue ball, or seeing the angles, can only be learned at the table. This book can help, but nothing can replace actual play and practice.

The speed at which you progress is directly tied to the amount of time you can devote to practice and competitive play. But because there are so many factors—aiming, stance, bridge, stroke, cue-ball control, and more—that in combination affect overall play, pool players virtually never experience the steady growth they expect. Instead, progress is typically experienced in periods of rapid improvement followed by nongrowth or stagnation. While these periods of nongrowth are unavoidable, it is nonetheless important that you continue to practice and look for improvements in your fundamental game.

A SOLID FOUNDATION

The most important factor in playing pocket billiards well is the complete understanding of all aspects of the game. You need not have mastered all areas of the game, but you must understand them and be aware of when and where they are used.

Let me offer an example. Many players feel that safety play (a defensive strategy for leaving your opponent without a shot) is a rather advanced concept. But it isn't. To play a safety, you simply use everyday skills (regardless of level) to place the cue ball and object balls in designated positions. It's exactly like any other shot but it does not involve pocketing a ball. If the concept of safety play is understood, most beginners can shoot a successful safety within their first month.

That is why you should learn about—if not necessarily perfect—every element of the game within your first month or two. Once you have a firm understanding of the game, you need only develop a good regimen of practice and play, and your game will progress.

Remember that since the advent of modern billiards (around 1845), no one has devised a theorem, formula, or system that has drastically affected the play of the game. Even opinions on stance, grip, and stroke have been proved wrong time and time again.

THE POOL TABLE

All tables have a name plate at one end that identifies both the manufacturer and the head of the table.

The head spot and foot spot are the dead-center positions in their respective halves of the table. The head spot has no functional purpose. The foot spot identifies the head position for a rack of balls.

The diamonds (circles or dots on some tables) are always spaced to divide the table perimeter in equal segments: eight on the long side and four on the short.

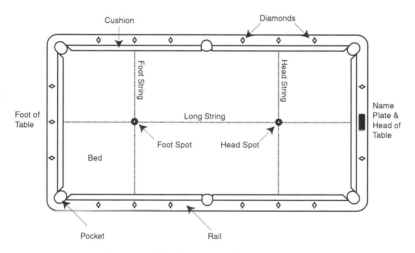

Important parts of a pool table. The head, foot, and long strings are all imaginary lines that run through the head and foot spots; they are used primarily for identifying specific areas of the table.

THE CUE BALL AND THE OBJECT BALL

The cue ball is the solid-white ball struck with the cue stick toward the object ball. The object ball is the numbered ball that you plan to strike with the cue ball. In most but not all cases, the object ball is the ball you intend to pocket.

THE MAJOR ASPECTS OF POOL

Four primary elements make up the complete game of pool: the shooting system, pocketing balls, cue-ball control, and the mental game. The shooting system includes the stance, grip, and stroke—all of the mechanics that go into shooting the ball. Pocketing balls is the act of shooting the cue ball in such a way that the object ball goes into the intended pocket. Cue-ball control is shooting the cue ball so that you can control where it lands after the shot, hopefully to make your next shot easier. And the mental game is learning to handle pressure and control your mind.

All of these elements will be discussed in more detail in the following chapters.

② THE SHOOTING SYSTEM ___

The term *shooting system,* which has been embraced by the Billiard Congress of America, refers to all of the mechanics that go into making a pocket billiard shot: stance, bridge, grip, and stroke.

Stance is defined as how you stand, holding the cue, as you address the ball. The *bridge* is the positioning of your front hand to stabilize the shaft of the cue stick. The *grip* is how you hold the rear end of the cue with the other hand. *Stroke* is the act of smoothly striking the cue ball with the cue stick. All of these components of the shooting system will be discussed in more detail later in this chapter.

I am among those who feel stance, bridge, and grip really don't matter very much as long as you're comfortable and can hit the cue ball consistently in the chosen place. There are many different styles being used successfully by both professional and amateur players of all levels. This should not be misunderstood to mean that the stance, bridge, or grip you use doesn't matter, because you must still strive to determine what works and feels best to you.

Of course, new players need someplace to start, so I will discuss all of the basic elements of a good shooting system.

DO THIS OR BE FOREVER AVERAGE!

Why are there so many average players in the world? Because they don't pay attention to their shooting system. It's not that they're intentionally negligent, they simply don't know any better. When they approach the table to make a shot, they have no idea how they're going to stand, what bridge they will use, or where they will grip the cue. They go with the flow— if it feels good, they do it.

If you want to reach your full potential, you must develop, refine, and memorize your shooting system. And you must use that system on every single shot.

Please note that the shooting system may, and usually does, have variables. For instance, you might grip the cue in one position for normal shots and farther back for break shots. Or you may use a closed bridge on normal shots and a V-bridge for rail shots. These variables are built into your shooting system, however, so that when you step up to a shot you immediately know what stance, grip, bridge, and head position to use. No need to fidget or fuss to find out what's comfortable.

The shooting system is the most important aspect of your game and consequently the most important topic in this book. Know it and use it from the beginning, and you'll be well on your way to becoming a fine pocket billiards player.

LEFT HANDERS AND RIGHT HANDERS

In the interest of simplifying my explanations of holding the cue, I'll refer to the *front hand* and the *rear hand*. For left handers, the front hand is the right hand and the rear hand is the left; for right handers, the front hand is the left hand and the rear hand is the right.

USING CHALK

Chalk is not just for advanced players who can do those fancy trick shots we all love to watch. Every player should use chalk on every shot—period! For more information on the proper use and application of chalk, see "The Cue Tip" on page 75.

SHOOTING SPEED

There are two basic types of players: the deliberate player, who takes time to study and set up each shot; and the fast and loose player, who appears to breeze around the table sinking balls in rapid succession. It's hard to get statistics on player speed, but personal experience shows that the deliberate types constitute roughly 80 percent of all players.

No doubt the reason that slower players constitute such a large majority is that this method is taught by virtually every instructor, book, and video. Fast players tend to be those who were self-taught and developed their style naturally.

You have no choice about which category you fall into. It is virtually impossible for a slow player to successfully convert to a fast player, and vice versa. And, in reality, it doesn't matter.

STANCE

Many experts now agree that any comfortable stance is acceptable so long as it achieves the following three objectives:

1. It places your head directly over the cue stick.
2. It allows you to freely move the cue stick.
3. It puts your cue, your head, and your right arm on the same plane with the line from the cue ball to the object ball.

In the classic stance, the back leg is straight or locked and the front leg is bent. But many excellent players stand with both legs locked, while others have both bent in what appears to be a crouch. Regardless of which position you finally choose, the end result should be comfort and stability.

Here's how to position your body for a classic stance:

1. With a cue ball on the table, hold the cue stick at the grip area and position the cue tip approximately 2 inches from the cue ball.
2. Stand erect, facing the cue ball squarely and with both feet together.

3. Move your left foot approximately 18 inches forward and to the left.

4. Adjust your feet for comfort, bend into position, and place the cue in a bridge made by your left hand.

Alignment of cue, right forearm, and eye on a plane with the cue ball

Another factor in your stance will be the position of your head in relation to your cue stick. Some players, like Willie Mosconi and Steve Mizerak, use a high head position with their chin 12 to 18 inches above the cue. This position offers a good view of the table, and shows you the relationship of all the balls along with the relative angle of the object ball to the pocket. Yet many other players today use a low head position, with their chin 2 to 6 inches above the cue. This is not normally a comfortable position the first time you try it, but many players feel it significantly improves their shotmaking by providing a better view of the relationship between the cue ball, object ball, and intended pocket.

BRIDGES

The bridge is formed by your front hand and is used to guide the shaft of the cue. There are two basic bridges: the V-bridge and the closed bridge. Actually, the V-bridge will work for every shot on the table, but many experts feel that the closed bridge provides more accuracy and control.

Regardless of which bridge you use, a good starting point is to allow about 6 to 8 inches between the cue ball and your bridge hand.

V-Bridge

The V-bridge is formed by placing your hand flat on the table, spreading your fingers slightly, and then elevating your thumb to form a V between it and the first knuckle of your hand. The cue is placed in this V.

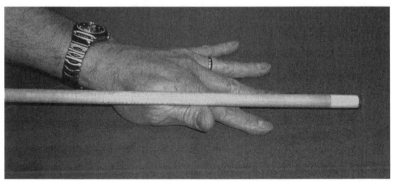

V-bridge

Maintaining the heel of your hand in a fixed position and moving your fingertips forward and backward will control the distance between the cue and the table, and subsequently where the cue tip strikes the cue ball.

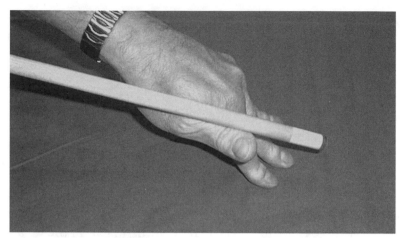

Elevated V-bridge to shoot over an obstructing ball

For shooting over balls, elevate your hand so only the fingertips are touching the table. The V-bridge is also ideal for shots where the cue ball is on or close to the rail, near pockets, and so on.

Closed Bridge

The closed bridge is formed by placing your hand flat on the table, spreading the fingers slightly, putting the tip of your index finger and tip of your thumb together, and then moving your thumb to the second finger. The cue is placed in the closed circle made by the index finger, thumb, and second finger. The circle can be adjusted so the cue fits snugly but can be moved freely.

As with the V-bridge, maintaining the heel of the hand in a fixed position and moving the fingertips forward and backward will help you control the height of the cue, and subsequently where the cue tip strikes the cue ball.

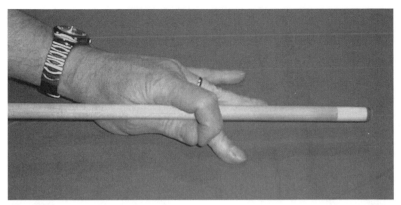

Closed bridge

Mechanical Bridge

The mechanical bridge is a device that is used when you cannot physically reach the cue ball with your normal bridge. The handle is the length of a cue stick. The grooves in the head of the mechanical bridge hold the tip end of the cue stick in much the same manner as your hand does in the V-bridge. Many players detest using them and have assigned the mechanical bridge nicknames such as granny stick and crutch.

Mechanical bridge

GRIP

The grip is the use of your rear hand to hold the butt of the cue. The best grip is normally a loose one, using only the fingers and thumb.

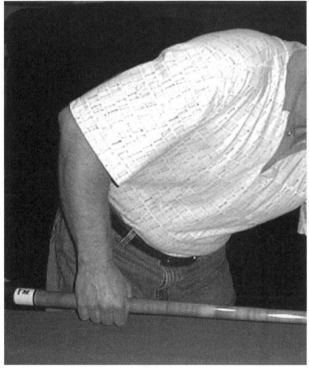

Right-hand grip

To determine where to place your grip hand, find the spot on the cue stick that causes your forearm to become perfectly vertical when in a shooting position with a level cue. Some players feel that a few inches forward of this position will give greater precision, while a few inches behind will offer more power.

STROKE

The stroke is the most important aspect of the shooting system. It is comprised of the practice strokes, shooting the cue ball, and the follow-through. When done properly, all aspects of the stroke are smooth and effortless.

Practice Strokes

The number of practice strokes before each shot varies from player to player, but three to five seems to be typical. During your practice strokes, you are glancing back and forth among the cue tip, cue ball, and object ball. This procedure ensures that you will hit the cue ball at the intended spot, and, in turn, that the cue ball will hit the object ball as planned. Practice strokes should be at the same speed that you intend to use for your actual shot.

Be sure your cue tip never touches the cue ball during practice strokes. If it does, the stroke is ruled a foul, and control of the table is turned over to your opponent.

Level Cue

It is universally accepted that, whenever possible, the cue stick should remain as level as possible through all phases of the stroke, thus ensuring that you will hit the cue ball where you aim.

You will see players, even professionals, who hold the butt of the cue in a high position. While this is not inherently wrong, it is risky. Most players who hold their cue high have a tendency to drop the butt of the cue on the final stroke, and consequently don't hit the cue ball where they aimed.

Follow-Through

Follow-through is the act of shooting "through" the cue ball, instead of jabbing or poking at it. As with many sports, the importance of follow-through cannot be overemphasized. Unless a specific situation dictates otherwise, on your final stroke the cue tip should extend 6 to 8 inches into the path of the cue ball.

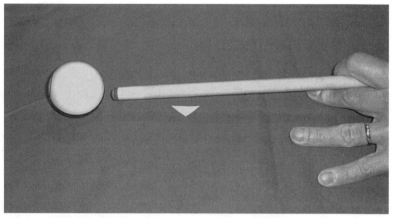

After a shot with good follow-through (the white spot shows the original cue-ball position before the shot)

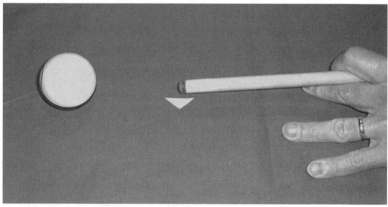

After a shot without follow-through (the white spot shows the original cue-ball position before the shot)

Why is follow-through important? Technically it's not, because the cue ball leaves the cue tip just milliseconds after being struck, and at that point all the follow-through in the world will not alter the shot. But by following through, you are ensuring that you're not stopping the cue stick at the very moment the cue tip should be striking the ball. For example, shoot a few draw shots with follow-through, and then shoot a few by just jabbing at the cue ball. You'll notice that the follow-through shots are much more effective and predictable. The nice thing about follow-through is that it's free, it can't hurt, and it'll probably help!

PUT IT IN WRITING

It's important to keep a written record of things you've tried and changes you've made in your shooting system. Otherwise, it will become impossible over time to remember all of your changes, experiments, and refinements, let alone if and how well they may have worked. A master sheet that describes every element of your current shooting system is an asset if your game should deteriorate.

Consider keeping a small card in your cue case that lists all of the key components of your setup and shotmaking. Then if (I should say when) things start to go wrong, go through the checklist and remind yourself of what you should be doing.

The Pre-pool Checklist

Perhaps I've saved the best till last. This final suggestion may give more consistency to your game than anything else in this book.

Each time you play, but before you open your cue case or step up to the table, describe to yourself your preferred shooting system. You can either carry an index card with you that lists the key elements or recall them from memory. By doing this, you will reestablish your goals. If you fail to do it, your mind will remember bad habits you've picked up and use them. The pre-pool checklist is like hitting the reset button on a computer—it clears out the bugs and restarts the system using good information.

Your shooting system will never be perfect. You must continually work to refine and improve it. Many experts feel that after you master the basics, it is the refinement of the shooting system that provides the most improvement to your game.

If your play should disintegrate, always return to the basics. The problem is more often in your fundamentals than in your aiming.

③ SHOTMAKING_____

Shotmaking is the essence of pool. Position play is important and will enhance your shotmaking, but if you don't make a shot, your turn at the table is over and good position becomes nothing more than a consolation prize.

The attitude of the best players toward making shots is a mixture of confidence and realism. They are confident of their ability to make any shot, but realize that they won't make all of them. And while everybody can accept missing the really tough shots, nobody wants to accept missing the easy ones.

KEYS TO SHOTMAKING

In its simplest form, the pool shot is made by using the cue stick to strike the cue ball toward the ball to be pocketed, called the object ball. The cue stick may only contact the cue ball in attempting a shot. Commonly, the cue ball is shot directly at the object ball, but it may also be shot at a ball that causes a chain reaction and ultimately makes the object ball. Such shots are explained later in this chapter.

Focus on the Object Ball

The one factor of overriding importance in making shots is that, on your final stroke, you must remain singularly focused on the object ball you intend to pocket. Your likelihood of missing is greatly increased if you make the shot while thinking about position play, English, or virtually anything other than sinking the object ball.

Staying Down on the Ball

Another important aspect of shooting is to keep your body and head in the shooting position until the cue ball comes into contact with the object ball. This is called staying down on the ball or staying down on the shot. If you're not disciplined to stay down, you can easily fall into the habit of rising to see the shot before you strike the cue ball. This almost always results in a missed shot or a miscue.

CENTER-BALL HIT

Each shot depends solely on how accurately you hit the cue ball—that is, whether you strike it where you intend. You must be able to execute a center-ball hit, hitting the ball dead center, with proficiency before you proceed to more complex shots. The center-ball hit is the foundation of a good game and the shot you must be able to fall back on when your game is not going well.

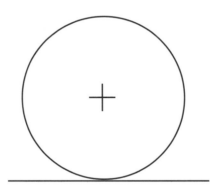

Center-ball hit

If you're new to the game you must concentrate on the center-ball hit until you can make it with consistency. Only after mastering center-ball hits should you attempt to learn advanced techniques of cue-ball control.

Here's a good way to evaluate and practice center-ball hits. Put the cue ball on the foot spot. Then, remembering not to move your cue stick after the shot, carefully aim and shoot the cue ball at the head spot with enough force to return it to the foot spot. With a perfect center-ball hit, the cue ball will return directly to the tip of the cue. If the cue ball veers off course to the left or right, this indicates that the shot was not exactly on center.

Don't expect to master center-ball hits quickly. It will take considerable practice before you perform these shots with consistency.

WALKING AROUND THE TABLE

If there's one thing that separates the good players from the also-rans, it's the time devoted to walking around the table, or studying the table (as it's also known). As the configuration of the balls gradually changes during a game, it's important that you always have a clear picture of the spatial relationship of the balls on the table.

Make it a habit to move around the table as you are shooting in such a way that you are constantly aware of the table layout. If several balls were moved on a shot, perhaps you should take the long way around to your next shot to evaluate the effects of their movement.

A major mistake made by many players coming off their chairs is going straight to the obvious shot. You will also see players do this after their opponent breaks. In either case, the player is planning to shoot with no real idea of the lay of the table. It is critical that you evaluate the entire table after a break or at the beginning of your turn. In no time this will become second nature, and your game will benefit noticeably.

AIMING SYSTEMS

It seems that everybody wants an aiming system. These systems are beginning to proliferate like exercise machine infomercials. The reason, of course, is that everyone wants to shortcut the practice cycle.

An aiming system is a technique for aiming the cue stick at the cue ball to hit the object ball at a specific point. Aiming systems are designed to make this process easier and more accurate. One such system has you visualize what fraction of the cue ball must contact the object ball to cause it move in the desired direction. Another requires you to use the side of the cue stick like a rifle sight to cause the cue ball to hit the object ball.

Many people are making money these days by marketing so-called revolutionary aiming systems. They're sold on the assumption that if you have an exact point of aim on the object ball, you'll hit it every time. I would submit that marksmen have very precise points of aim on their targets, plus incredibly accurate sights on their rifles, and yet struggle with their ability to execute perfect shots. The problem is not pinpointing the target, but controlling the shot.

I have tried every system available. They all resulted in fewer balls pocketed than when I used only my natural instincts.

If a specific aiming system is the answer to our problems, then why is it that long straight shots, which require no aiming system whatsoever, can present the greatest challenges? Again, the answer is simple. It's not the point of aim, it's the execution!

There is only one effective aiming system in use. It involves learning where to hit the object ball with the cue ball to make it move to a specific location (normally a pocket). Practice of and familiarity with the various types of shots develop an intuitive sense of aim.

STRAIGHT SHOTS

To the novice, straight shots appear the easiest. However, straight shots, especially long ones, can be among the most challenging and should be practiced frequently.

If the shot is truly straight in, one technique is to shoot as if you're trying to put the cue ball in the pocket, ignoring the object ball altogether. If, however, the cue ball and object ball are both at the far end of the table from the desired pocket, it is often easier to find your point of aim within the pocket. This reduces the margin of error associated with aiming at a close object that must travel a long distance.

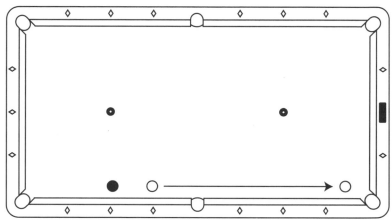

Straight-shot practice technique

Many pros begin each practice session with straight-shot practice, as shown above. They shoot short straight shots, then gradually work up to full table-length shots.

CUT SHOTS

Cut shots are by far the most common type you'll encounter. The term *cut shot* refers to any shot of a single object ball at an angle, rather than straight in.

Cut shots can be made at any angle greater than 90 degrees. Although a 90-degree cut shot is not for the faint of heart, it is possible if you cause the cue ball to contact the object ball with the thinnest possible hit. To learn to recognize if a cut shot is makable—90 degrees or more—envision two imaginary lines: one from the pocket through the center of the object ball, and another from the side of the cue ball that would contact the object ball to the point on the object ball farthest from the pocket. If the lines you created form more than a right angle (90 degrees), the shot is possible.

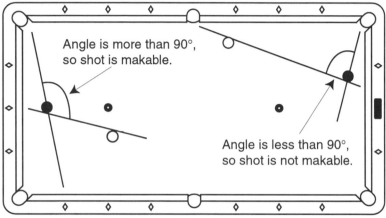

Angle is more than 90°, so shot is makable.

Angle is less than 90°, so shot is not makable.

Determining if a cut shot is possible

All of us have certain cut shots that give us problems. Perhaps we fail to practice a particular shot; when we see it, it appears odd, and we lack a point of reference on which to base our shot. When faced with any shot in which you lack confidence, make a note to include such a shot in your next practice session.

The diagram at top right depicts a table layout for practicing cut shots. With five object balls placed at equal distances between the foot spot and the cushion, and the cue ball placed a few inches from a side pocket, attempt to make each object ball. Begin with the object ball closest to you, and return the cue ball to its original position after each shot. As the diagram shows, this simple drill provides a complete range of makable cut-shot angles.

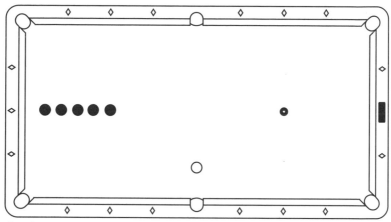
Cut-shot practice technique

As your shotmaking improves, practice pocketing the balls in reverse order, beginning with the farthest ball. And finally, the drill can be made even more difficult by placing the cue ball near one of the corner pockets at the head of the table.

I would guess that you can already make some easy cut shots, and that you can or will very soon be able to make some of the difficult ones. Then you only need to realize that every cut shot on the table is a variation of those you can already make. Life is good!

RIGHT-ANGLE RULE

The right-angle rule is the most important and most often used in all of pool. Understanding the right-angle rule is critical for shotmaking at all levels of play. In the next chapter I'll deal with cue-ball control in much greater detail, but for now, the right-angle rule explains the movement of the cue ball after impact—and therefore is the foundation for position play.

The right-angle rule says that on a cut shot, the cue ball will deflect at a 90-degree, or right, angle from the path of the object ball. This, of course, is of critical importance in determining where the cue ball will stop.

There are two deviations from this rule. If the cue ball has forward roll, or "follow," on it when it strikes the object ball, the angle will be 10 to 15 degrees less than a right angle. If the cue ball has "draw," or reverse roll, on it when it strikes the object ball, the angle will be 10 to 15 degrees more than a right angle. Draw and follow are discussed in further detail in "English" on page 54.

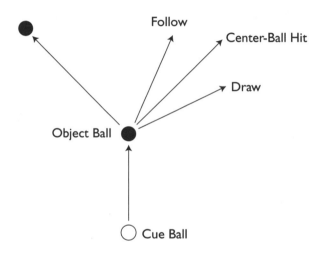

Effects of follow and draw on the right-angle rule

BANK AND KICK SHOTS

The difference between a bank shot and a kick shot is whether the cue ball contacts the object ball before or after it contacts a cushion. In a bank shot, depicted on the left half of the table at top right, the cue ball first contacts the object ball, which is subsequently banked into the side pocket. In a kick shot, depicted on the right, the cue ball contacts the cushion and then kicks the object ball into the corner pocket.

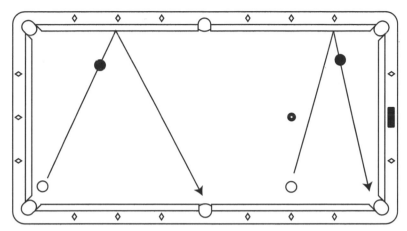

The shot on the left is a bank shot; on the right, a kick shot.

In very general terms, a ball will depart a cushion at the same angle at which it approached. However, for this to be true, the shot must be made at a medium speed without English, draw, or follow. This is what makes bank shots so difficult.

Because of the extreme variability of bank and kick shots, it's best to used them as shots of last resort.

As with most aspects of pocket billiards, the best way to learn how to bank is to practice. After several hours on the table shooting nothing but banks and kicks, you'll gain a feel for the angles.

But many players need a more concrete system to get started, and if you're one of them, the diamond system may help you visualize bank shots.

THE DIAMOND SYSTEM

In the diamond system—the most common method of predicting bank shots—you use the diamonds or dots on the rails to help you see the results of a bank. The system's basis is the symmetry of approaching and departing angles. While the diamond system is better than nothing, it's no more than a rough guide.

Diamonds

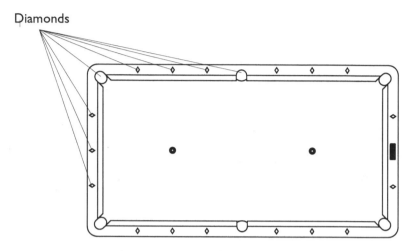

There is also a diamond at each pocket.

When you're using the diamonds to make bank shots, use the diamonds themselves, not the points on the cushion closest to them.

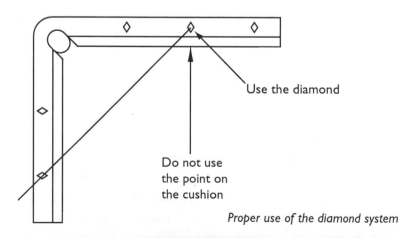

Use the diamond

Do not use
the point on
the cushion

Proper use of the diamond system

The diamond system helps you establish banking angles that are equal. In the table layout below, the diamonds are used for reference so you can visualize banks that will work.

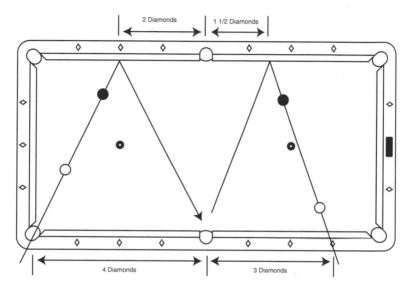

Bank shot running the width of the table

To determine the proper bank point for the shot in the left half of the diagram above, you must locate a line that runs through the object ball that runs half the distance from the side pocket on the upper rail as it does from the side pocket on the lower rail. The line in this example is 2 diamonds from the upper side pocket and 4 diamonds from the lower side pocket. With a medium–speed shot, the bank should work.

If you apply the same formula to the shot in the right half of the above diagram, you'll see that you can locate an intersecting line running through the object ball 1½ diamonds from the side pocket on the bank rail and 3 diamonds from the side pocket on the lower rail.

Applying the same formula to a bank shot that runs the length of the table, you'll find it works exactly the same. In the diagram below, the intersecting line is 2 diamonds from the foot rail and 1 diamond from the head rail.

This formula (although it sometimes requires fractional distances, such as 1½ diamonds) will provide the equal angles you need for a bank shot. Because of the variations possible in

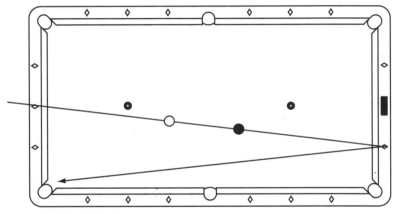

Bank shot running the length of the table

ball speed, you will find the diamond system to be less than exact, but it will help you get close while practicing and developing your eye.

COMBINATION, CAROM, BILLIARD, AND KISS SHOTS

Combination, carom, and billiard shots all involve two or more object balls. The order in which they are struck, and which ball is finally pocketed, determines the type of shot.

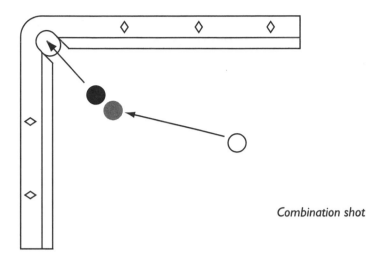

Combination shot

A combination shot uses a chain of two or more balls to pocket the last ball in the chain. In the above illustration, the cue ball hits the gray ball, which in turn sinks the black ball into the corner pocket.

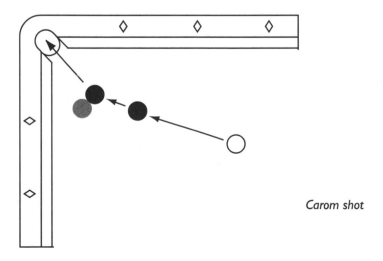

Carom shot

In a carom shot, the object ball caroms off one or more secondary balls on its way to the pocket. In the illustration on page 37, the cue ball strikes the black ball, which then caroms off the gray ball and heads into the corner pocket.

In a billiard shot, the cue ball caroms off one or more secondary balls, putting the object ball in the pocket. In the following illustration, the cue ball billiards off the gray ball and in turn sinks the black ball in the corner pocket.

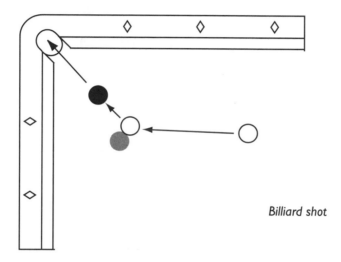

Billiard shot

Carom, combination, and billiard shots warrant some practice, but they don't come up frequently, and their many possible variations make it impractical to practice them in great detail.

In a kiss shot, you are attempting to pocket or "make" one of two balls that are frozen together. A kiss shot can be made when the imaginary line that runs between the two frozen balls is perpendicular to a line through their centers and leads straight into a pocket. In such a situation you have a lot of latitude in where you can hit the ball to be pocketed. Here's a typical kiss-shot scenario:

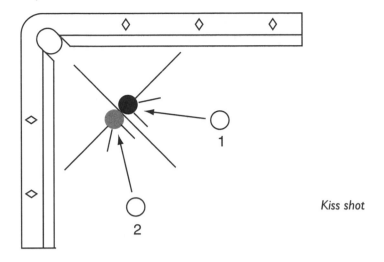

Kiss shot

You can make either the gray ball or the black ball, depending on the position of the cue ball. If the cue ball is located in the general vicinity of position 1, shoot to hit the black ball anywhere between the two short lines and the black ball will be pocketed. If the cue ball is located in the general vicinity of position 2, shoot to hit the gray ball anywhere between the two short lines and it will be pocketed.

Note that the actual position of the cue ball doesn't matter as long as you hit the respective ball between the two short lines. Practice will demonstrate the actual points indicated by the short lines, but shooting to make the the ball as if the kissing ball was not there will result in a pocketed shot.

TROUBLESHOOTING

What went wrong? Everything was going along so well. You were making shots and getting good positions when all of a sudden the roof fell in. There are two likely explanations.

Fundamental Breakdown

A slump or lack of progress is most often related to the fundamentals—a breakdown in the shooting system.

Golfers in a slump often run out and buy a new set of clubs. While pool has its share of players who head to the cue store every time there's a problem, more often we blame our aim. It must be our aim that is keeping us from hitting the object ball properly. But is it?

If you are addressing a shot and are unsure of how to make it, then you may have a problem with your aim. If that is the case, get on the practice table and work on the shots that are giving you trouble. Your problem should be corrected in short order.

But most of us will have the opposite experience. We know how to make the shot and are sure it's going to sink, but it doesn't. When this happens a lot, you're in a slump.

It's easy to change your stance inadvertently, hold your cue in an unlevel position, or fail to follow through your shot. Often, a series of unusual shots can give rise to bad habits. For example, if you're faced with a series of four or five shots where the cue ball is on the rail, this requires you to elevate your cue and doesn't allow you to follow through. When confronted with the next normal shot, you may not automatically return to that nice level stroke with follow-through that you worked so hard to perfect.

Now for the good news. Remember that small card in your cue case that I discussed in chapter 2? Step up to the table and, reviewing this card item by item, take a few shots. If you notice that things feel different, even slightly different, by using this card, you've most likely found the answer to your problem.

Perhaps the best way to deal with such problems is prevention. Get in the habit of telling yourself what you expect before each pool session. Before you ever throw a ball on the table, talk yourself through your desired shooting system. Use that little card if you like, but do it before you do anything else. This tells your brain what you want instead of allowing it to repeat mistakes you may have made in your last outing. After all, if you can just prevent the replication of mistakes, it won't be long before you are shooting a pretty darn good game of pool.

Law of Averages

Another possible answer to the question of what went wrong is that the law of averages is at work. Just as it's possible for an intermediate player to run three racks, it's also possible that you're going to have a game or two in which nothing goes right.

The bottom line is that transitory factors such as fatigue, illness, and lack of concentration occasionally affect your game and must simply be taken in stride and forgotten.

4 CUE-BALL CONTROL _____

The great Ray Martin once said, "Pool is very simple. Just sink one ball after another, and make sure each time that your cue ball stops where you have an easy shot!"

Cue-ball control and position play are virtually the same thing. Actually, good position play is the result of good cue-ball control, but you'll hear the terms used interchangeably. Another similarly used term is *cuing,* which is the act of hitting the cue ball to achieve a specific effect. Look at it this way: If you're cuing the ball well, you'll have good cue-ball control, which will result in good position play.

Cue-ball control can be as simple as varying the speed of a shot or as complex as adjusting speed and skid while applying English to the cue ball. Regardless of the technique involved, though, cue-ball control means shooting the cue ball so that it stops at a designated point after it strikes the object ball(s).

Cue-ball control is a prerequisite for pattern play, which I'll discuss in the next chapter. Pattern play is a method for determining the most effective sequence of shots based on ball positions on the table. It goes without saying that knowing this sequence is of little use if you cannot control the cue ball's position.

SPEED CONTROL

Controlling the speed of the cue ball is, of course, an important step toward cue-ball control. Your brain must learn the difference between hitting the cue ball to move it 6 inches, and hitting the cue ball to move it the length of the table.

Most players develop a sense of cue-ball speed in the normal course of practice and play. However, many novices and some more experienced players find controlling speed to be difficult. If you need help with speed control, or if you're just looking to refine your control, the following exercise may be helpful.

Medium Stroke Speed

The first thing you want to do is determine the stroke required for a medium-speed shot. I will define a medium-speed shot as similar to a lag shot. A lag shot is made by placing a ball near the head spot and shooting just hard enough to bounce it off the foot cushion and return it to the head rail.

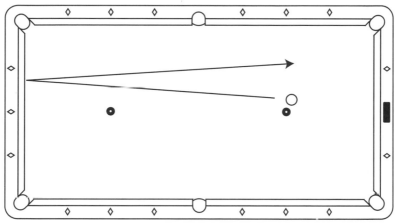

Medium-stroke-speed drill

A center-ball hit should be used for all shots. Place the cue ball on the head spot, and shoot it hard enough to make it bank off the foot rail then return to, and stop at, the head rail. Make this shot a few times just to get warmed up, then several more times until you are comfortable with your ability to place the cue ball consistently within 1 diamond of the head rail (this exercise is obviously more difficult for new players). You are now ready to expand your speed control.

Advanced Speed Control

The second phase of the speed-control exercise will help you get a feel for the stroke speeds necessary to deliver the cue ball to various parts of the table. You'll learn to stop the cue ball at points 1 diamond apart along the length of the table. Remember that the two corner pockets and the side pocket are also at diamonds.

Begin by making several shots trying to make the cue ball bank off the foot rail then stop 1 diamond short of the head rail. Then repeat, but change your target to 2 diamonds short of the head rail. Repeat this procedure, each time moving 1 diamond closer to the foot rail, until finally you are shooting to make the cue ball stop at the foot rail.

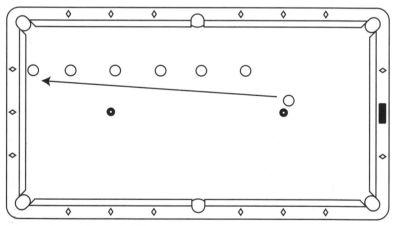

Advanced speed-control drill

If you assume that your original lag shot is a medium stroke, you can consider the shot to the foot rail to be a light stroke. You've now learned everything from medium to light over 8 diamond increments. If desired, you can also use the same technique to establish very light shots, those that stop short of the foot rail; or harder shots, those that go several diamonds past the head rail.

This exercise is not easy and you shouldn't get discouraged. But if you can learn to perform such feats with relative consistency, you will have excellent speed control.

Adding the Object Ball

Thus far I've discussed speed control for a cue ball alone. Now you have to use this information to make shots wherein the cue ball contacts an object ball. To mark the ball positions as required in the following exercises, use chalk or small pieces of tissue paper under the balls.

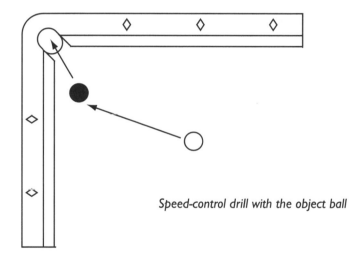

Speed-control drill with the object ball

Set up a cut shot near a pocket, mark the position of both balls, and make a test shot using a medium stroke. Mark the spot where the cue ball comes to rest. Now try varying your stroke in 1-diamond increments. Repeat this several times, varying the cut angle and the cue-ball-to-object-ball distance. Very soon your brain should begin helping you hit the desired target point on every shot.

SKID

Skid is a term that describes the phenomenon of the cue ball skidding across the table, instead rolling across it, based on how hard it was struck with the cue stick. As you will find in the demonstration that follows, a hard shot can cause the cue ball to skid for several feet before it begins to roll. Conversely, with a soft shot the cue ball will begin rolling almost immediately. Skid is a relevant factor when you wish to apply spin or English to the cue ball, because spin cannot take effect until the cue ball has stopped skidding.

On every shot, the cue ball skids across the cloth for a short distance before friction causes it to begin a forward roll. The speed of the shot determines how far the cue ball skids. On a very soft shot, the skid may be less than ¼ inch; on a harder shot the cue ball might skid for several feet. Thus draw is ineffective after the cue ball has stopped skidding, because at that point it has begun a forward roll. Follow can be used to counteract skid by causing the cue ball to begin a forward roll almost immediately upon impact by the cue tip.

To see how skid affects a center-ball shot, place any striped ball on the head spot, as in the diagram below, so the stripe is exactly parallel to the bed of the table.

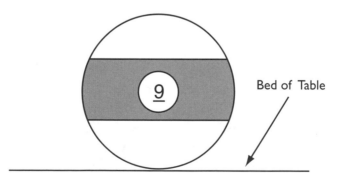

Bed of Table

Placement of the striped ball to test cue-ball skid

Use the striped ball in this orientation as a temporary cue ball. Shoot it toward the foot spot at varying speeds to see the effects of skid. During the skid portion of the shot, the stripe will remain parallel to the table bed, but as friction takes over and the ball begins to roll, the stripe will roll end over end.

THE STOP SHOT

An essential component of cue-ball control is the stop shot—one that causes the cue ball to stop dead at its point of impact with the object ball. The stop shot can only be accomplished straight in.

The key to stopping the cue ball dead in its tracks is to execute a center-ball hit with enough force that it is never allowed to begin rolling forward before it strikes the object ball. In other words, it skids all the way to the object ball. This causes all of the energy of the cue ball to be transferred to the object ball and, in turn, the cue ball stops dead.

When the cue ball and object ball are more than 1 or 2 feet apart, it may not be possible to stop the cue ball with a center-ball hit. In such cases applying a little draw (hitting below center) will extend the effective range of the stop shot.

To recap, a stop shot requires a perfectly straight shot and a perfect center-ball hit. Since even the pros cannot always do this with certainty, don't expect to be able to execute a perfect stop shot each time. You should be satisfied if the cue ball drifts less than 2 or 3 inches to one side or the other.

Stop-Shot Exercise

Set up an object ball 1 diamond from a pocket. Place the cue ball approximately 1 diamond from the object ball to form a straight-in shot.

Use a center-ball hit and medium speed to see if you can achieve a stop shot. If things don't work out in a couple of tries, the following paragraphs may provide some help.

As I discussed earlier, a stop shot is only possible when the shot is absolutely straight in and the cue ball strikes the object ball before it stops skidding and begins to roll. If the cue ball strikes the object ball at even the slightest angle, however, it will drift at a 90-degree angle for a short distance to the right or left. If this happens, try again to perfect a straighter hit.

On the other hand, if the cue ball stops skidding before impact, it will roll forward slightly after striking the object ball. If this happens, try again but increase your speed to make the cue ball skid farther.

ENGLISH

English, which is accomplished by hitting the cue ball off center, is used to change the course of the cue ball after it contacts the object ball or a cushion. English can be broken down into three categories: follow, draw, and left or right spin.

Because a center-ball hit is always the safest and most predictable, English of any kind should be used only when necessary. Beginners should concentrate on center-ball hits. And all players should avoid English until they are reasonably proficient at shotmaking.

The mistake that many players make is thinking they need to move their cue tip farther away from center than is actually necessary. As you will see, you can apply plenty of follow or left/right spin simply by moving the distance of 1 cue tip from the center in the appropriate direction. This means that one edge of your cue tip will be immediately adjacent to the center of the cue ball. Draw requires a drop of 2 tips below center for maximum effect.

The cue-ball diagrams that follow are proportionally correct. They show the center spot on the ball so you can get an accurate picture of exactly where to place your cue.

FOLLOW AND DRAW (ENGLISH)

By using *follow* (hitting the cue ball above center) or *draw* (hitting the cue ball below center), you can change the movement of the cue ball after it hits the object ball.

The following diagram demonstrates where the cue tip should strike the cue ball to cause either follow or draw action on it.

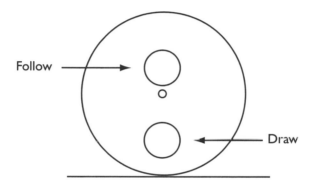

Cue-tip point of impact for follow and draw

As the names imply, follow causes the cue ball to follow the object ball after it is struck, whereas draw will draw the cue ball back.

Follow and draw also alter the angle of the cue ball after it hits the object ball. As you know, after being contacted by a center-ball hit, the cue ball will move in a 90-degree angle to the path of the object ball. When you apply follow, the cue ball will move at less of an angle (approximately 75 to 80 degrees). When you apply draw, the cue ball will move at more of an angle (approximately 100 to 105 degrees). Do some experiments and you'll soon see the advantages of follow and draw in position play.

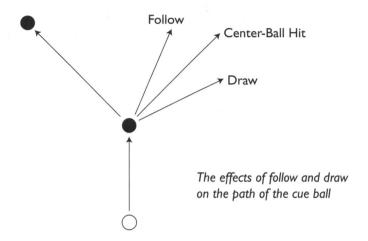

The effects of follow and draw
on the path of the cue ball

Recipe for a Draw Shot

New players can go for years without developing a decent draw shot. This is indeed a shame, because draw shots are not particularly difficult. They just require attention to detail. Here are the four building blocks of a good draw shot:

1. Use chalk!
2. Hit the cue ball low, perhaps lower than you think possible.
3. Keep the cue level, using your bridge hand to adjust the elevation of its tip.
4. Follow through.

I'll assume that chalk requires no further explanation and discuss the other three items on the list.

Many players just refuse to hit the cue ball as low as needed to produce an effective draw shot. Look again at the cue-ball diagram on page 49. It is not an exaggeration. Draw is not like follow and English, whereby you simply help the cue ball move in a natural direction. Draw requires you to make the cue ball spin in an unnatural direction and hence requires a very low hit. The first thing to try if your draw shots are not up to par is to hit the cue ball lower than you think is safely possible.

Unless unusual factors dictate otherwise, you should strive to maintain a level cue when attempting to draw the cue ball. If the butt of your cue is elevated, it will cause the cue ball to skip or jump instead of spin in reverse. If this happens, the best you can hope for is a stop shot. By the same token, the reason for lowering the bridge is to allow you to hit the cue ball low and level. If you maintain your bridge in a normal shooting position while attempting a draw shot, you've no choice but to elevate the butt to hit the cue ball low.

Many players think they must jab at the cue ball to make it draw. Doing so will produce erratic results—a nice draw on one shot, then no draw at all on the next. To produce a consistent draw on the cue ball, the cue tip must stay in contact with the cue ball long enough to produce backspin. Follow-through produces consistent contact, whereas a jab is totally unpredictable.

Follow and Draw Exercise

Before beginning this exercise, set up your cue ball and an object ball as in the diagram on page 52. Shoot some stop shots to establish the speed you need to pocket the ball in the side pocket and to stop the cue ball dead. In the following exercises, be sure to chalk before every shot.

To produce a follow shot, use the same ball positions and the same stroke as on the stop shot, but move your cue tip 1 tip above center, as in the diagram on page 49. When you shoot now, instead of the cue ball stopping, it should follow the object ball into or near the far side pocket. Repeat the follow shot several times to see if you can get the cue ball to follow into the far side pocket.

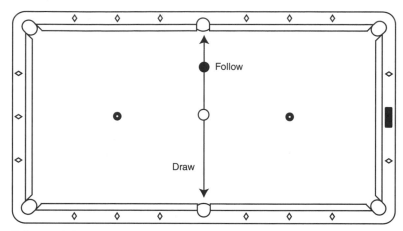

Follow and draw exercise

For a draw shot, use the same ball positions and the same stroke as above, but this time move your cue tip down to the draw position. Lower your bridge, check that your cue is level, and remember to follow through. This time, when you shoot the cue ball should contact the object ball and then reverse direction, ending up in or near the closer side pocket. Repeat the draw shot several times to see if you can get the cue ball to draw into the near side pocket.

Once you are comfortable with your ability to produce follow and draw, set up cut shots on a corner pocket. Observe the effects of follow and draw on cut shots at various angles.

The Effects of Speed on Follow and Draw

In both follow and draw, softer shots decrease the cue ball's angle of deflection off the object ball, while harder shots increase the cue ball's angle of deflection. See the two diagrams opposite for examples.

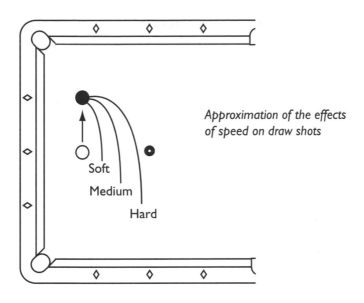

Approximation of the effects of speed on draw shots

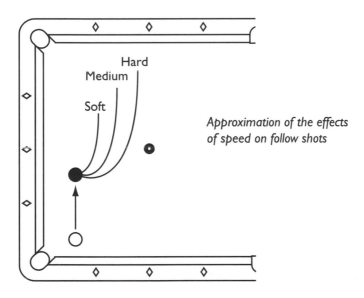

Approximation of the effects of speed on follow shots

LEFT AND RIGHT SPIN (ENGLISH)

Most top players can move the cue ball around the table to their satisfaction without using English. They prefer not to use English, in fact, because it complicates a shot. As I'll discuss under "Squirt" and "Curve," it is impossible to impart English and have the cue ball move in a straight line from your tip to the object ball.

There are, however, times when English is essential for a specific shot. Left spin or right spin, also referred to as left or right English, is imparted by hitting the cue ball at any point left or right of center. Shown below are the approximate maximum limits of striking the cue ball without miscuing; you can strike the cue at points between its center and this maximum point to vary the effect.

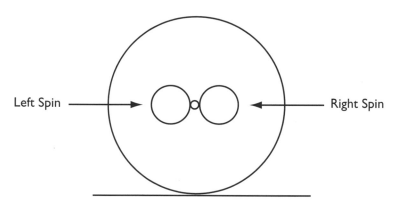

Cue-tip point of impact for left and right English

Keep in mind that the most English you will ever need is just 1 cue tip to the right or left of center, such as in the above diagram. And often much less than 1 tip of English is adequate. Many professionals limit their use of English to just ½ tip. They feel that this offers the desired effect without unduly complicating the aiming process.

Although English has many subtle uses in advanced play, the primary use of left or right spin is to affect the path of the cue ball after it contacts a rail. The following diagram shows such effects on the path of the cue ball.

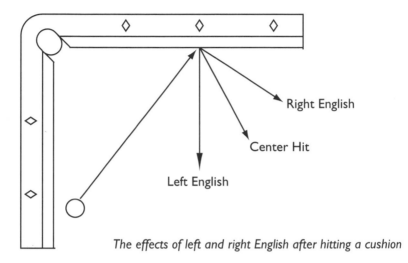

The effects of left and right English after hitting a cushion

Note that the cue ball is approaching the cushion from left to right; right English will thus lengthen the angle, and left English will shorten the angle. If the cue ball was approaching the cushion from right to left, the reverse would be true.

English Terminology

You may hear of other types of English. There is reverse and running English, and there is inside and outside English. Both of these sets of terms use different words to describe the same thing—that is, reverse and inside English are the same, as are running and outside English.

In the above diagram, look at the path of the cue ball to the rail. Left spin applied to the cue ball is also known as reverse or inside English, because you're using English on the inside of the angle and to the reverse of the normal path of the ball. Conversely, right spin applied to the cue ball is also known as outside or running English, because you're using English on the outside of the angle and running with the normal path of the ball.

The Effects of English on Aim

You cannot hit the cue ball to the left or right of center and expect it to follow the same path as a center hit. Two factors known as squirt and curve come into play. These must be considered and compensated for during the aiming of a shot using sidespin.

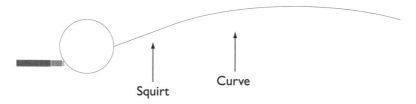

Squirt

Curve

This is exaggerated to show effect.

Squirt

The laws of physics dictate that when a perfectly round object (the cue ball) is struck with a small object (the cue stick), it must move away at an angle of 180 degrees, or directly away from the point of impact. In pocket billiards, this effect is called squirt. Squirt comes into play when you apply left or right English and the ball moves away from the cue tip, but not necessarily in the direction in which the cue stick is pointed. This is only natural when you think about it. See the diagram above for details.

To see how squirt affects aim, place the cue ball on the foot spot and make several shots at medium speed using left or right spin, aiming directly at the head spot. Unless you are subconsciously compensating for squirt, which good players learn to do, you will consistently miss the spot. Also experiment with speed; you'll find that softer shots are less affected by squirt.

Curve

Obviously, left and right English cause the cue ball to spin. Once it stops skidding, the spin against the felt will cause the cue ball to curve back toward the line of the shot. See the diagram at left for details.

Only spin that is applied above or below the center point, or horizontal axis, of the cue ball will cause the ball to curve. This is because English applied on the horizontal axis has the effect of making the cue ball spin in place.

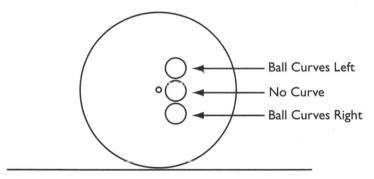

Ball Curves Left

No Curve

Ball Curves Right

Cue-ball curve positions

To see how curve affects aim, place the cue ball on the head spot and make several shots at medium-slow speed, using left or right spin in combination with follow or draw, aimed at the foot spot. After traveling a foot or so, the cue ball should gradually curve back in the direction the spin was applied. Speed is a factor; the amount of curve is greater with slower shots. You may also want to make the same shots with left or right spin only. You'll notice that no curve results.

CHEATING THE POCKET

Don't worry, you aren't really cheating! As you know, a straight-in shot does not offer many opportunities for position play. Cheating the pocket is simply a technique for using the extra space in the pocket to shoot a straight-in shot at a slight angle.

You can cheat the pocket anytime the object ball is within a foot or so of it. If draw or follow alone will not get you the position you need, make the shot as a very slight cut shot. Just plan it so that the object ball goes in the pocket, but there's enough angle when the cue ball hits the object ball to give you a deflection to the right or left.

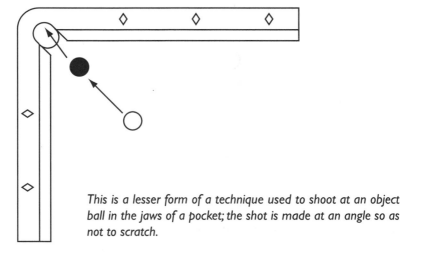

This is a lesser form of a technique used to shoot at an object ball in the jaws of a pocket; the shot is made at an angle so as not to scratch.

⑤ ADVANCED PLAY_____

SAFETIES

Playing a safety, or playing safe, is making a shot whose only purpose is to leave your opponent with an impossible situation, rather than trying to pocket a ball. Ideally, a safety leaves you in control of the position of the balls on the table; you don't miss a difficult shot and leave your opponent in control.

The point of this section is not to teach you safeties. You don't really learn to play safeties; you merely learn to recognize the times when they are preferable to difficult and low-percentage shots. The point is not how to play safe, but when to play safe.

Always remember that a safety is an available option. If you are faced with a low-percentage shot (a shot you make 50 percent of the time or less), always weigh the possible benefits of shooting a safety.

You will find that your safety play will progress along with your normal game even if you never specifically practice it. This happens because safeties are a normal extension of regular play, in which you shoot at an object ball and try to gain position on the cue ball.

The unique facet of safeties, though, is that you are called upon to be creative. Since there is no single place you want the object ball to go, you have endless options. Of course the ideal option is giving your opponent a shot that forces him to leave you in good position. Safety play can become a chess match within a pool game.

BREAK SHOTS

The break shot is the opening shot for all popular pool games. It is made with the cue ball behind the head string and the object balls racked on the foot spot.

In the most common games today, 8-ball and 9-ball, the break shot is a power break in that you want to pocket as many balls as possible and spread any remaining balls around the table.

The following are the points to be considered in developing a good break:

• Shoot as hard as possible while still remaining in complete control of your cue stick.
• Strive to have the cue ball come to rest in the middle of the table.
• Use a center or low-center hit on the cue ball to kill it at the point of impact.
• Make a solid hit on the apex ball (the ball resting on the foot spot). To determine the aim point for a solid hit, sight a straight line from the desired cue-ball position to the apex ball.
• Grip the cue 3 to 6 inches closer to its butt than normal.
• Stand more erect, with your feet slightly farther apart.
• Use a closed bridge to maintain control of the cue.
• Lengthen your stroke 2 to 3 inches for break shots.
• Stay down on the shot. Of all the shots, it is easiest to raise your head on the break.
• Always chalk up. A miscue on a break is disastrous.
• A break cue, if used, should have a stiff shaft and a hard tip. This cue (described in chapter 7) is simply a separate cue reserved for breaking so as to spare your normal cue from these punishing shots.

You cannot with any degree of consistency control where the object balls will land on a break shot, but you can to some extent control the cue ball. The diagram at top right shows the ideal cue-ball position after the break for any game that requires a power break.

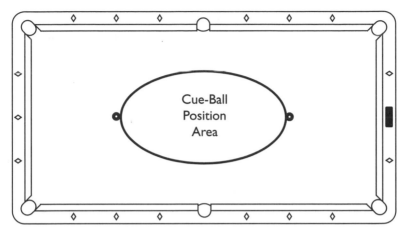
Ideal cue-ball position after the break

JUMP SHOTS

A jump shot causes the cue ball to become airborne and fly over ball(s) that are obstructing its path to the object ball. It is accomplished by holding the cue at a 30- to 45-degree angle and shooting down on the cue ball slightly below its center, as in the diagram below. Because your cue tip is headed straight for the cloth, your follow-through must be shortened to ensure that the cue tip does not contact the table and rip the cloth.

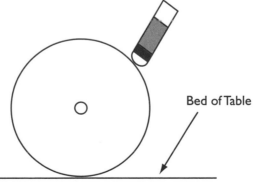

Bed of Table

Proper cue position on a jump shot

Jump shots are very difficult and obviously put the cue ball out of control. Because of this, a jump shot is always the shot of last resort. Never consider a jump shot when a safety is available.

Jump shots have become popular in the past few years since they were made legal in 8-ball and 9-ball play. When done properly, they are exciting to see.

However, jump shots are dangerous. Now, I'm not going to turn into your mother and tell you, "You could put somebody's eye out!" But you can certainly cause a nice long, irreparable gash in the cloth. And we both know who gets to pay when that happens.

At the very least, if you are going to learn or practice jump shots, go to a billiard room. Explain to the proprietor what you want to do and ask if he has a table that he plans to re-cover in the near future. Thus if the cloth is damaged, it isn't a big deal.

As an alternative, find a pool table installer and ask for a scrap of cloth about 6 inches square. Put the scrap underneath the cue ball to avoid any damage to the cloth. Note that this is not the best option, because a piece of cloth laid loosely on the table does not act like cloth that is fastened and under tension. But it's better than nothing.

PATTERNS

A pattern, or pattern play, as applied to pocket billiards, is the ability to establish the most advantageous sequence of plays to run a table of balls. Whole books have been written on recognizing patterns and planning shot progressions to pocket balls in a pattern.

Cue-ball control and position play, as discussed earlier, are critical skills in playing patterns and sequences. Recognizing patterns is of little use if you don't have the ability to move the cue ball accurately through the desired sequence of shots.

If you play only 9-ball or rotation you can skip this section, because in these games you must shoot the balls in numbered order and consequently have no control over the sequence.

K.I.S.S.

You remember this old acronym for "Keep It Simple, Stupid." If you followed some methods for determining pattern play, you'd stand a 50-50 chance that your opponent would die of old age while you attempted to read the table. Let me see if I can simplify the whole issue of pattern play to make it manageable and, possibly, fun.

In the following diagram is a typical table with 14 randomly placed balls. Instead of thinking in terms of patterns for a moment, examine the table for sets of balls that are grouped in such a way that they can be made in a short sequence. The balls here have been labeled in groups A, B, and C, indicating one possible solution.

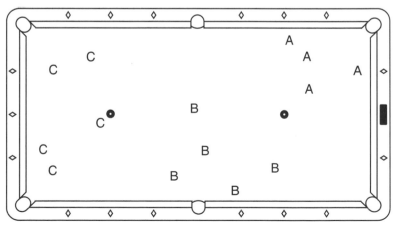

Pattern play

Now, depending on the location of the cue ball, select the group you would like to eliminate first. Then determine which ball in that group you want to shoot last in order to move into position for the next group.

That's all there is to it: Simply establish groups, then eliminate each, leaving a preselected last ball for position. All without the use of slide rules, protractors, or highly paid mathematical assistants.

An important point about this type of pattern play is that you always want to eliminate all the balls in a group before you move on to the next. The last thing you want is to be left with three or four balls scattered all over the table.

CLUSTERS

Clusters are groups of three or more balls that are touching or very close to one another. True clusters must be broken up in order for the individual balls to be pocketed.

Before assuming that a cluster must be broken, though, study it to be sure that it doesn't contain several relatively easy shots. The diagram at top right shows what might appear to be a cluster, but in reality is four very makable shots. If shot in the numbered sequence, and using good position play, each ball can be pocketed in a corner without ever disturbing the adjacent ball(s).

Some players try to make the breaking of clusters look like some sort of mystical sleight of hand. It isn't. Breaking a cluster is no more than position play. You simply want to control the path of the cue ball (as you do on all shots) so that it contacts a group of balls. Now, was that so hard?

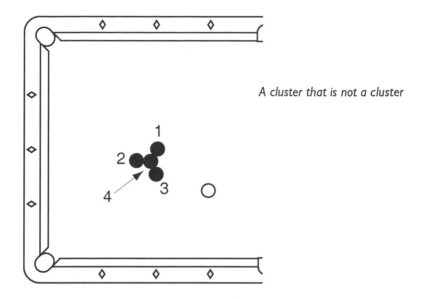

A cluster that is not a cluster

ADVANCED CUE-BALL CONTROL

I cannot discuss advanced position play without also men-
tioning the need to plan ahead. It is an accepted practice to
plan at least three shots in advance. This means considering
your current shot plus the next two balls you intend to pocket.

Everyone can understand the need for planning the
current shot plus the next one, because you must get into
proper position to make the second shot. But why the third
shot? You must know how you're going to shoot the third
shot to make the proper position play on the second.

Take a look at the diagram on the next page. Ball 1 will be
your next shot and a center–ball hit will provide natural position for ball 2. But if you don't think ahead to ball 3, you
could easily shoot hard enough to send the cue ball into the
area marked B. This would require a terrible shot on ball 2 to
get into position for ball 3.

By looking ahead to ball 3, though, you can see that the
area marked A would provide ideal position for pocketing ball

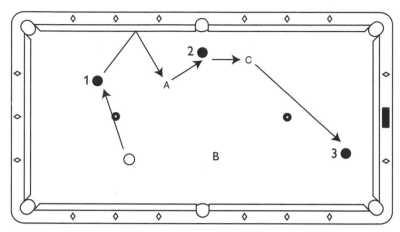

Thinking ahead on position play

2 and getting into position on ball 3. All you have to do is use a slightly softer stroke on the same center-ball hit.

As you become more experienced, you will no doubt begin to plan farther ahead. Most experienced 8-ball and 9-ball players have a pretty good idea of their entire shot sequence before ever taking their first shot after the break.

SPIN COMBINATIONS

True mastery of cue-ball control comes with the combination of vertical-axis spin (follow and draw) and horizontal-axis spin (left and right English). These provide you with the tools to always place the cue ball in an advantageous position. Applying left follow, right follow, left draw, or right draw is as simple as selecting a position on the cue ball that is between the horizontal and vertical axes.

The key to ensuring the best possible position play is to always plan for the cue ball to have an angle on the object ball, because straight-in shots limit your options and all but eliminate the effective use of left or right spin.

Once you begin to learn advanced position play, you want

to give yourself plenty of room for success. While Willie Mosconi claimed he could predict cue-ball position within 2 inches after any shot, for most of us this would be a recipe for frustration. When predicting cue-ball position after a shot, give yourself a nice-size area of the table. A section 2 diamonds square is often sufficient, and a 1-diamond square should accommodate all but the toughest shots. By giving yourself more room to succeed, your confidence in your position play will grow rapidly.

POWER WHEN YOU'RE READY
In the hands of a player who has taken the time to learn and practice the use of English, it is a powerful weapon. The cue ball can be made to move around the table in seemingly magical ways. But the learning curve is steep and the frustrations are many.

After you begin to study and experiment with cue-ball control, your level of play may drop slightly. This is, no doubt, due to the fact that you have complicated your shooting system. While your game will come back stronger than ever, you should carefully pick the correct time to begin any new technique.

⑥ TRAINING THE BRAIN_____

In many ways pool is the perfect game. Assuming you play on a decent table (and why would you do otherwise?), you face no obstacles that are out of your control. Other games have sand traps, weather, injuries, poor officiating, and the like, which can alter the outcome of the game. Pool has none of these.

The bad news is that this makes you 100 percent responsible for the outcome. Pocket billiards is a mind game, pure and simple. Your success relies totally on the training and ability of your mind. Consequently all of the blame for failure must also rest squarely within yourself.

But maybe this isn't such bad news after all. Just think: Only one thing stands between you and greatness, and that one thing is totally within your control.

LEFT BRAIN/RIGHT BRAIN
Some of the most fascinating scientific discoveries of the past two decades have involved the understanding of the two hemispheres of the human brain, the left and the right. I will offer a brief explanation as it applies to billiards.

Science has found that the left brain is largely responsible for analytical matters, while the right brain handles creative processes and spatial relationships.

Now I can hear you saying, "I got it! Pool is analytical. Therefore it is handled by the left brain." Not really. While you must rely on your left brain to make certain calculations, it is the right brain that is responsible for your best play.

You may have heard the terms *dead stroke* or *being in the zone*. These describe a player who is essentially on autopilot. He simply looks at the shot that needs to be made, looks at the position to be played, and the brain does all the calculations and tells his body how to execute the shot.

Most experts now agree that when a player is in dead stroke he is most likely playing under the direct and total influence of his right brain. The right brain has seen all the shots hundreds of times before and simply responds by telling the body how to carry them out.

Similarly, your right brain is responsible for position play. In fact, one professional who is noted for his precise position play has recently confided that he does no more than look where he wants the cue ball to land and then forgets about it and makes the shot. In essence what he is saying is, "Okay, right brain, here's what I want. So when I get ready to shoot, take care of things."

If you're skeptical, perform the following test. With all the numbered balls off the table, put the cue ball on the foot spot. Now shoot the cue ball to the other end of the table so that it stops within a foot of the rail. If you didn't get it on your first shot, try a few more times.

Note that in the above test, there were no formulas, or any instructions you could use to accomplish the shot. Willie Mosconi himself could not tell you how to do it. The only way to make the shot is for your brain to know what you want and then give your body the appropriate instructions. If you've never made the shot before, the chances are good that you were way off. If, however, you've made this or similar shots many times, you probably came pretty close on your first effort.

If you're still not willing to accept this, just try to imagine the alternative: On each and every shot you'd have to go through an incredibly complex series of calculations and computations of angles, banks, speeds, and table factors, which in turn you'd have to transfer to your arm. Not likely!

Think of it this way. Your left brain is like a database that understands $2 + 2 = 4$, half of a right angle is 45 degrees, and a cue ball will veer away from an object ball at a 90-degree angle to it. Conversely, your right brain is the computer software that is being continually programmed with every shot you make. It can take a shot you've never made before and figure the correct angle based on similar shots you've made in the past.

HOW TO IMPROVE

There is only one way to get better at pocket billiards. Through systematic practice, train your brain to recognize certain shots and then, when needed, let your brain tell your body how to execute them. This is true of every shot that can be made on a billiard table.

Visualize the Shot

I noted above that you must tell your right brain what you want. This is done through visualizing, or seeing the shot.

The ideal preshot scenario has you visualize the shot you'll make along with the path or position of the cue ball. By doing so you are telling your brain exactly what you expect and giving it all the information it needs to accomplish the task.

IT'S NOT WHO YOU PLAY, IT'S HOW YOU PLAY

It doesn't matter who you are playing; to win you need only make all the balls during your turn at the table.

That statement is simple and true. Your opponent might be the guy from the gas station, the lady from the bank, or the current world champion of pocket billiards. It doesn't matter.

Regardless of who your opponent is, as long as you are pocketing balls, he sits and watches.

There is no other game that gives you such control and leverage. It reduces all of your opponents to one level. Thus to worry about who you are playing is a waste of time and energy. This alone should boost your confidence.

There is, however, one other factor. Competition does strange things to our minds and bodies. Just walk into a tournament and your mind can shut down; your body reduce to a tired, nervous shell. You have no idea who the guy was who thought this might be a good idea, but he sure isn't here now.

I don't know what causes this phenomenon, but there are some ways to get past it. Two closely related techniques seem to work for the vast majority of players. Relaxation and self-hypnosis are both practiced widely in all forms of competition, but are so introspective that you never know when they are being practiced.

CONCENTRATION

This should be the shortest section in the book, because you cannot control concentration. Trying to concentrate harder is like trying to grow faster. And telling someone else to concentrate is just as futile.

Concentration is an inner state of the brain, which is either focused or not. The best you can do is use relaxation techniques (described below) to clear some of the clutter away and provide the brain with positive images. In turn, this can allow for more concentration. But don't waste your time trying to force yourself to concentrate.

RELAXATION TECHNIQUES

Your mind can only think about one thing at a time. Therefore, if you focus on relaxation, the mind is cleared of negative thoughts and the body is brought back into a normal state.

One of the most accepted methods of coping with pressure is to focus on breathing. Sit down, if possible, and feel the sensation of long deep breaths. This is especially helpful while watching your opponent at the table or even in between your own shots.

Whole-Body Relaxation

Whole-body relaxation can be more difficult, but it's a good exercise, especially before and between matches. Here's how it's done. Sit down, set your cue aside, and keep your hands apart. By setting it down, you can't grip it—which actually creates tension. And by keeping your hands apart, you refrain from clenching, gripping, wringing, or other tension-building habits. If you recognize other nervous habits such as biting nails or tapping feet, try to adjust your body to avoid them.

Focus on breathing for a few minutes. Then relax your legs and notice how good they feel. Relax your arms, shoulders, and neck, and concentrate on how good they feel. When you're finished, your body should be completely relaxed and your mind very refreshed.

Self-Hypnosis

While much has been written about self-hypnosis, it is really a very simple process and does not involve hypnosis at all. Self-hypnosis is merely a combination of relaxation and positive thought reinforcement.

The idea behind a self-hypnosis session, which can take as little as two to three minutes, is to control your breathing, relax your body, and then tell yourself what you want to achieve in positive terms. Here is a quick self-hypnosis session that you might use before a match or practice session:

• Sit down in a comfortable position with your arms and legs uncrossed.
• Focus on breathing, and take 5 to 10 slow deep breaths.
• Beginning with the extremities, slowly relax your whole body.

Silently say or read the following statements (substitute as desired) to yourself:

• I am going to have fun playing pool today.
• I am going to stay relaxed as I play.
• I am going to stay focused on the game.
• I am going to maintain my shooting system on every shot.
• When I am not shooting, I will relax and enjoy the atmosphere.

Notice that there's no talking of winning or losing, or making or missing shots. These are pressure-inducing terms that you want to avoid. What you're doing is putting yourself in a frame of mind to play your best game. That in and of itself will help you to win and enjoy it!

ADDITIONAL INFORMATION

There are many good books and videos on the various techniques I discussed above. I encourage you to take a look at them and then experiment to find out what methods work best for you.

7 EQUIPMENT

CUES

When you're selecting a cue stick, the most important thing is how it feels in your hands when you're hitting the cue ball. In that regard it is just like a tennis racket, golf club, or baseball bat.

Butt   Wrap   Forearm   Joint   Shaft   Ferrule   Tip

The parts of a cue

There are two types of players when it comes to cue sticks: One is comfortable shooting with any piece of straight wood that has some leather on the end; the other is very sensitive to the specific feel of each different cue. These are personality differences only, and have nothing to do with quality of play. There are good and bad players in each group.

If you don't already know which group you fit into, shoot a few balls with a variety of cues. If you didn't notice any difference, or at least none that matters to you, then you're in the "any stick will do" group. If, however, you felt specific differences and perhaps had a preference for one cue, then you are in the "sensitive" group.

Cue selection for players in the "any stick will do" group is greatly simplified. Just find a cue that looks good and is within your budget, and start sinking balls. But before you run off with your credit card in hand, the following sections may be useful.

The "sensitive" group will find selecting the right cue to be slightly more formidable. It is, however, an enjoyable task, because it will ensure that you get the very best cue for your personal taste. You will find all of the remaining sections useful, but "Selection" was written specifically for you.

The Cue Tip

The size, shape, and condition of the cue tip are among the most important factors in pocket billiards. Unfortunately, many players fail to fully consider tip size when buying a cue. And still more fail to properly maintain the cue tip during its use.

The cue tip can be 12 to 14 millimeters in diameter. The most common size is 13 millimeters, but many experienced players prefer a 12- to 12.5-millimeter tip.

Put serious thought and experimentation into determining your preferred tip size before you purchase a cue. While it's possible to have your shaft diameter reduced, and ferrule and tip replaced, it's obviously better and cheaper to get it right the first time.

Regarding the tip itself, if you don't like the one that comes on a new cue or have become accustomed to another brand, have it replaced before you take the cue home. Many dealers will do this at little or no charge when you purchase a cue.

The condition of the cue tip can have a profound effect on your game. Inspect the tip every time you take the cue out of its case, and periodically as you play. It should have a convex shape with the approximate curvature of a nickel; its surface should be slightly rough.

A properly shaped tip on the left, and a worn tip on the right

Chalk is applied to the tip of the cue before each shot to provide friction between the tip of the cue and the cue ball. When applying English, this prevents the cue from sliding off the cue ball (a miscue).

To properly apply chalk, hold the cue stationary and gently brush the chalk over the curved surface of the tip. The tip should have a light but even layer of chalk; the chalk should never appear caked or packed on the tip.

Tips do not last forever and must be replaced occasionally. A fairly active player who shoots five or six times a week can expect to replace tips every four to six months at a minimal cost.

Leather Tips

The traditional cue tip is made of cowhide leather, although buffalo leather is becoming increasingly popular. You can select from a range of hardnesses for either type of leather tip.

Leather tips do require routine maintenance. It is normally necessary to reshape the tip to maintain its convex shape, and to scuff it so that chalk adheres, before each playing session.

Composition Tips

Synthetic or composition tips, such as Future Cue Tips™, are made from a polymer material. They have several advantages:

• They last many times longer than leather tips.
• The intervals between reshaping and scuffing sessions are many times longer than with leather. Composition tips can endure many weeks of heavy play with no such maintenance.
• They can be transferred from one cue to another.
• Because they don't deteriorate as fast, hits are more consistent and reliable.

And there are disadvantages:

• The price of composition tips is about double that of leather.
• The hardness range does not closely coincide with that of leather tips.

A few final notes on composition tips. After years of using a variety of brands of leather and buffalo tips, I now use composition and probably won't return to leather. If you're thinking of switching to composition, begin with a medium hardness (normally blue). Virtually every composition-tip shooter I know uses it. Most players feel the harder tips are much too hard, and the softer ones seem to deviate too far from the feel of a natural leather tip.

Cue Weight

Cues can weigh between 18 and 22 ounces. The average cue weight for professionals is 19 to 19.5 ounces. One ounce can make a great difference in the feel of a cue, so be selective with your first purchase.

Many cues have a built-in bolt system in the butt that allows the weight to be changed easily. These are ideal for the beginner who is not sure which weight he prefers.

Don't make the mistake of the many beginners who want the heft of the heavier cue. Guys should beware the macho attitude that more weight is better because you're "man enough" to handle it.

The Shaft

The feature to be aware of in the shaft is its flexibility. Some cues now use 10-piece spliced shafts that are extremely rigid and have little flex when they impact the cue ball. Other cues with traditional solid-maple shafts are highly flexible, which some players feel provides superior cue-ball control. The flexibility of the shaft will be most noticeable on medium to hard shots.

Balance and Feel

Balance and feel are actually two distinctly different characteristics, but the terms are often used interchangeably. Balance can be measured. By using a fulcrum, you can establish the balance point of any cue. Feel, on the other hand, is simply a personal judgment of how the cue feels in your hand. Two cues with the same balance point and weight can feel quite different.

Once you have established your requirements for weight and tip diameter, the feel of the cue is the most important factor in your selection.

Is It Straight?

It goes without saying that you don't want to buy a warped cue, but in the heat of the moment it is easy to overlook one. Unfortunately most cues do not come with a warranty of any type, so if you should take home a warped cue, it's most likely yours to keep.

Of course the old standard for checking a cue's straightness is to lay it on a pool table and roll it. This will detect major flaws. But a better and more precise method is to sight down the cue. Hold the butt of the cue near your face and, with the cue tip away from you, roll the cue slowly as you sight down its length. Even minor imperfections will be immediately apparent.

Appearance

The choices of cue appearance are endless. You can select from exotic wood with Irish linen wraps and gold inlays, fluorescent colors with wildlife scenes, and synthetic materials like graphite and aluminum.

While some players want to make a statement when they remove the cue from its case, appearance should be the last consideration. As hard as this may be to swallow, the cue is your only weapon in the battle to sink balls, so performance must be your primary objective.

Remember, the gallery will remember who won the match, not who had the most impressive cue.

Where to Buy

There are two major requirements for a good cue dealer: a large selection, and a pool table on which you can try various cues before making a purchase. Such dealers are normally willing to spend as much time as necessary to help you make your decision. They understand that your satisfaction is imperative to their business and therefore are not interested in pushing any particular cue.

Ideally such a dealer will do repairs on site, will provide tip replacements while you wait, and will often trade cues.

But keep in mind that such dealers are not discount houses. They provide a valuable service and in return must demand full price. I urge you not to use them to find the cue you like and then make your purchase from a discounter.

If you can't find a good dealer in your area, check the local billiard rooms to see if they rent cues. By renting various models over the course of several visits, you should be able to establish your preferences.

Selection (Without Regard for Price)

The ideal selection process would allow you to choose from all available cues with total disregard for price. While the downside of this is finding that the cue you love is totally out of your price range, the upside could be finding a cherished stick for less than $100. Either way, you will learn a lot from the process.

I'll assume that you've found a good dealer with a nice selection of cues. I'll also assume that he has a decent table you can use. With such dealers, you may get better service by making an appointment, thus ensuring the attention you deserve. Keep in mind that you don't have to be spending big bucks to get this kind of attention from a good dealer. He will gladly help you select an $80 cue to foster a long-term relationship.

There are several factors you should determine before you start the selection process. You should know your preferred price range, cue weight, tip diameter, and type of wrap (leather, linen, or none). If you aren't sure of preferences, your dealer can help you with those decisions before you start the selection process. I will call these preferences your basic criteria.

But trying all of the cues at some dealers would be challenging. My dealer has over 500 in stock. Trying each of them is impractical. So with his help, I established a method that allows general selection by brand, followed by a more specific selection by individual cue.

Let's say you go to your dealer shopping for a cue in the $200 to $600 range. Explain to him that you want to do a blind trial—where, as much as possible, you don't know the brands or prices of the cues you're using.

To begin, ask him if you can try one cue from each manufacturer whose cues fit your basic criteria. Your basic criteria will determine how many brands qualify.

Now the fun begins. You want to make a few shots with each of the various cues the dealer has selected for you. The goal of this process is to find two or three brands for which you have a strong preference. Here are a few pointers before you get started:

• The actual number of shots you take with each cue will most likely depend on how good it feels. Inferior cues will be rejected with one or two shots, while cues that feel good will demand more attention.

• Before using a cue, make sure its tip is properly shaped and chalked. Before reshaping a tip, ask the dealer if he prefers to do it or if he wishes you to do the reshaping.

• Consider not making actual shots, but instead shooting the cue ball around the table. Since the idea is to determine how the cue feels hitting the cue ball, trying to pocket balls under these conditions is merely a distraction.

Once you have selected a small group of brands you prefer, you want to try other cues within those brand names that fit your basic criteria. I'll assume you have selected two brands that really appeal to you. I'll call them brands A and B.

Try all of the available cues from brand A that fit your basic criteria. Select the one or two that you most prefer and set them aside. I'll call this group the finalists. Repeat the procedure with brand B.

From the cues in the finalist group, you simply find the one that you want to use for the rest of your life. Obviously, at this point you may find two cues that feel so much alike you can't tell the difference. Let price and appearance be your determining factors.

Now you should be able to ante up your credit card and walk out of the showroom with reasonable assurance that you have selected the best cue available. But what if you still have some gnawing concerns? Here are some options to consider if you're not completely comfortable with your decision:

• Ask the dealer if, based on the cues in your finalist group, he has other cues that he feels you should compare to your final selection.

• Take a stroll around the showroom and pick out a few cues that really strike you, based on appearance alone. Compare your final selection to the cues chosen off the rack.

• Find another dealer. Perhaps you stumbled into a Yugo dealership, but you're looking for a Mercedes. Don't buy a cue just because you went out to buy a cue. Buy a cue because you are thrilled with what you found and are more than willing to pay the price.

Price

Ah, the price! Cues range from $30 to over $10,000, and they all do the same thing. If you ask how much you have to pay for a good cue, the answer is about $150. But if you ask if $4,000 is too much to pay for a cue that makes you feel good when you're playing, gives you confidence, and in fact makes you want to play more, the answer is absolutely not.

Cues are analogous to cars. A Cadillac and a Chevette will do the same thing—move you from point A to point B. One person is thrilled owning a Chevette, because he's found reliable transportation at a minimum price. Another is thrilled to own a Cadillac, because it makes her feel good and she enjoys driving it. Obviously, both made the right decision.

When you shop for a cue and need to specify a price to yourself or the dealer, consider stretching your budget to the absolute maximum. While I am not advocating spending more than you could or should, I do know that it's a sad fate to tell the dealer you can't spend over $500, then later find that the cue of your dreams was never considered because it had a price tag of $550. No one can force you to buy an expensive cue, but it sure is a shame not to consider all of your options.

If you find a cue so superior in feel that it virtually has no rivals and yet is out of your price range, I urge you to either wait until you can afford it or try some creative financing.

Explain your plight to the dealer and ask if he has any options to offer. Perhaps he has a layaway program and will loan you a used cue until yours is paid off. The point is that you don't want to let a very special cue get away and forever wonder what your game would have been like had you owned it.

Storage

When not in use, your cue should be stored at normal room temperature and humidity and in such a way that it will remain flat and straight. Moderate temperatures and low humidity are the best defense against warping. Consequently, never store your cue, even for short periods, in a car trunk. If you store your cue in a case most of the time, humidity-absorbing desiccant packages are very effective.

Any good hard case will work well, as will a place to hold the cue in a vertical position. Soft cases are best hung so that the cue remains vertical.

Cue Cleaning

With the possible exception of the tip, cues are very low-maintenance items. If yours should get dirty, a wipe with a damp cloth followed by a dry cloth is all that's needed.

Here's a tip that may help during play. If your cue shaft starts to feel tacky in your bridge, go to the bathroom and wash your hands, use a couple of paper towels to dry them, and then use the damp paper towels to clean the shaft. The cue will slide through your fingers as if it were new. In the past, billiard rooms typically provided powder for players to dry their hands, but in recent years, in an attempt to keep the tables cleaner, many owners have begun to frown on the use of powder.

Cue Repair

Most cue repairs are best left to a professional; they often require special equipment not normally found in the home workshop. If you don't have expert cue repair in your area, return your cue to the manufacturer to be assured a professional job.

There is, however, one technique useful for smoothing minor dings or ripples in the shaft that is safely performed almost anywhere. If you should encounter a rough, rippled, or bumpy area in the shaft, simply use the side of a smooth water glass (it must be smooth glass) and, with medium pressure, rub the area back and forth until the defect is gone or improved.

Special Cues

Before you read on and get all excited about the various special cues that I'm about to discuss, let me note that many great players use only one cue in all circumstances. They feel it is better to be intimately familiar with one cue. Again, you must decide what is best for your game.

Break Cues

Many professionals now use a break cue for break shots in games that require power breaks (8-ball and 9-ball). Break cues are typically the same weight or slightly lighter than your normal cue. Break cues are used because it is felt that the forceful hits of breaking put undue stress on the joint (the point where a two-piece cue screws together), and also causes compression of the tip. Most experts agree that the ideal break cue:

• is 2 to 3 ounces lighter than your normal cue.
• has a stiff shaft.
• has a hard cue tip.

While owning a separate cue for breaking is very popular, there are still many players who prefer to break with their shooting cue. Still others use a house cue for breaking, thus obviating the need to purchase another cue. You make the call!

Jump Cues
Jump cues are shorter and lighter versions of regular cues designed to jump the cue ball over balls in its path.

Sneaky Pete Cues
A Sneaky Pete is a two-piece cue designed to look like a house cue. They are often used by hustlers or those who want to look like players of lesser skill. Sneaky Petes cost $50 to $125 and can be made to your specifications.

Cue Accessories
In addition to the accessories I'll mention below, you may want to consider carrying your own chalk with you. If you're wondering why you should pay good money for something poolrooms give out for free, there are two reasons.

Many times the chalk provided by an establishment is less than ideal. Chalk that has absorbed high levels of humidity or skin oil will cake unevenly on the cue tip instead of providing a uniform coating of powder. On many occasions I have had to waste time in search of a decent cube of chalk.

Perhaps a more practical reason is to preempt an opponent who likes to hide, move, or lose the chalk that should be at the table. This is basically a sharking ploy that you can prevent by simply having your own cube of chalk in your pocket.

Tip-Maintenance Tools
There are a variety of inexpensive tools on the market for maintaining the shape and texture of the tip.

Cue-tip shaper

The tip of a cue should have a convex shape with the approximate curvature of a nickel. It should also be slightly rough so that it will hold an even layer of chalk. Tools such as the one shown above make it easy to maintain the proper shape and texture of the tip.

Cue Cases

Unless you plan to play only in your home, you will need a case for your cues. There is a large variety of cases that will protect your cue(s) well. Since nice cases can cost over $100 and are designed to hold a fixed number of cues, it's best not to go overboard on the case until you've decided how many cues you will routinely be carrying. It's also a good idea to ensure that your case has enough room for all those accessories you carry around.

Shaft Conditioners

Sometimes I think shaft conditioners, such as Cue Silk™, are one of the great inventions of my lifetime. This is a clear thick liquid that is rubbed into the shaft of the cue in very small amounts—four or five drops per application—and dries instantly. It completely eliminates the need for powder, even on sweaty hands, because it makes the shaft as smooth as silk.

TABLES

Most tables found in billiard rooms or available through reputable dealers meet the specifications of the Billiard Congress of America. These are minimum standards that mandate pocket size, bed dimensions, height, and so forth. This, however, is often not true of tables found in bars, bowling alleys, or similar venues.

A standard commercial pocket billiard table

A regulation table is called a 9-foot table and measures 9 feet by 4½ feet. Eight-foot tables are also popular and can be sanctioned for use in leagues and tournaments. There is also a 7-foot table, but it is not often found in billiard rooms and seldom used for serious play.

In the table layout on the next page, note the nameplate at center right; this always indicates the head of the table. Outside dimensions are approximate and vary by manufacturer, but interior or bed dimensions are exact.

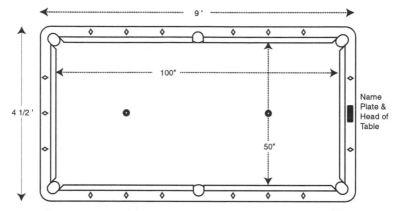

Layout of the table

Buying Your Own Table

There are two categories of billiard tables available: home and commercial. And while the two may look similar, commercial tables have smaller pockets and wider rails, and are generally more sturdy.

Current prices range from $1,500 for an 8-foot home table to $6,000 for a top-of-the-line regulation commercial table. These prices *do* include installation and all accessories—balls, house cues, chalk, and so on.

There are two types of people who wish to purchase a billiard table: the casual player who wants a table for family recreation, and the serious player geared toward competition and tournament play.

The casual user will probably consider a home-type table. These are much less expensive ($1,500 to $4,000) and yet can offer a lifetime of enjoyable play.

The serious player should consider a commercial table, however, because such tables are the norm for billiard rooms and tournament play. While there are many subtle differences between home and commercial tables, perhaps the most important is that commercial tables have smaller pocket openings. Regulation corner pockets must measure between 4⅞ and 5⅛ inches at the opening. The pockets on most home tables measure 5⅛ inches, but those pockets on commercial tables normally measure 4⅞ inches. While both are regulation, the ¼-inch difference will significantly affect the way each table plays.

It can be detrimental to your game to practice on a home table and then play competitively on a commercial table. If you cannot own a table similar to those you will play on in competition, it makes sense to practice where you play.

Room Dimensions

The primary consideration in deciding to purchase your own table is space. In short, you must allocate space for the table itself plus 5 feet on each side for cuing a ball that is against the rail.

Billiard Table Dimensions and Space Requirements			
Table Size	Regulation	Play Area	Min. Room
9' x 5'	Yes	100" x 50"	220" x 170"
8' x 4'	No	88" x 44"	208" x 164"
7' x 3.5'	No	80" x 40"	200" x 160"

Cloth (Practice Fast, Play Slow)

Cloth is the single most influential factor in how a table plays. One cloth can make the balls mope around the table like they're on tranquilizers, while another can make them seem like rockets careering off the cushions.

Whether you practice at home or at a billiard room, it is important to practice on a table that is equal to or greater in speed than the table you would play on in any serious game, competitive or not. For most players, it is easier to adjust to a slower table than to a faster one.

The proper selection of cloth lets you adjust the speed of your table. There are many brands and varieties of billiard cloth, but I'll discuss only Simonis, because that's what is used to cover most professional tables.

Simonis 860 cloth is probably found on more tables than any other cloth. It is a very durable worsted wool-nylon blend and it's an excellent choice for any table. It comes in a variety of colors.

Simonis 760 (available only in green) is a faster cloth. It is also a worsted wool-nylon blend, but not quite as durable as the 860. Since tournament tables are normally covered with 860 that has seen substantial use (and hence is faster), selecting 760 for your home practice table provides a fairly good speed match.

You should plan to spend $100 to $200 (installed) to cover or re-cover a table with Simonis or other premium-grade cloth.

Table Covers

Most tables are supplied with a plastic cover. Obviously, one of the reasons to use a cover is protect the table from dust and dirt when it's not in use.

If your table is in a room that receives any natural sunlight, though, perhaps a more important reason to use a cover is to protect the cloth from the sun's damaging rays. Direct sunlight will fade the cloth, most likely in an uneven pattern, and soon your beautiful table will look like it's covered with old army fatigues. For this reason, do not use any type of see-through plastic as a table cover in a sunlit area.

I should note that I have experienced problems with both types of commercially available table covers. The cheap plastic kind can emit an objectionable odor that can permeate a billiard room. And the expensive Naugahyde covers have a white spun-filament underlining that can come off and adhere to the table cloth. Both of these situations are unnecessary annoyances.

I have found that a better and less expensive way to cover the table is with the cotton broadcloth found in fabric stores. It is available in 120-inch widths. This means a single 2½-yard piece will cover any 9-foot table. By hemming, on both sides, you have a very nice cover for less than $20. And experience has shown that cloth is much easier to handle and more durable than those other popular products.

Cleaning the Table

Cleaning the cloth on your table is important, but don't overdo it. It's certainly not necessary to brush it before every use. Limit cleaning to when the cloth is visibly dirty.

Use a table brush for cleaning. Most tables come with one. Brush with the nap of the cloth (from head to foot), and don't forget the cushions and under the cushions.

Do not use a vacuum cleaner on your table. These tend to stretch the cloth and are very hard on it.

The wood or laminate portion of the rail may need an occasional cleaning with a damp cloth. Do not use cleaners or polishes on this area, because you must touch the rails for some shots; cleaners can leave sticky residues, while polishes often make the surface slick.

The Final Word

Perhaps the best advice I can give you about owning a pool table is not to use it for any other purpose. Turning your table into a battleground for GI Joe, a cocktail buffet for the Christmas party, or a makeshift workbench is a disaster waiting to happen.

BALLS

As with most things in life, there are billiard balls of various qualities on the market. The best-quality balls, such as Brunswick Centennial, which cost about $150 per set, have the following advantages:

- They will last longer.
- They will play truer.
- They are easier to clean.
- When cleaned and waxed, they will keep their shine longer.

Needless to say, billiard balls take quite a pounding. And because they become dirty from handling and chalk, it is advisable to clean and wax them about once a week to maintain truly predictable play. There are products on the market specifically designed to clean and wax balls in one step. You can achieve similar results by wiping the balls clean with a damp cloth, applying a good liquid car wax with a damp rag, and, when dry, buffing with a clean cotton cloth.

8 RULES OF THE GAMES _____

The following rules are commonly accepted in most areas of the United States, but are not the official rules as published and copyrighted by the BCA, and may vary from room to room. For a complete set of the official billiard rules, contact: The Billiard Congress of America, 1700 First Avenue, Suite 25A, Iowa City, IA 52240.

GENERAL RULES FOR ALL GAMES

The following rules apply to all games unless altered or amended in a specific game's rules.

Lag for Break

Unless otherwise noted, the first game of any match is determined by a lag for break. To lag for break, each player selects a solid ball (not the cue ball, unless cue balls are provided for all players) and places it behind the head string. Both players simultaneously shoot their ball toward the foot of the table; the player whose ball returns closest to the head rail wins the lag.

The winner of the lag may elect to break or pass the break to his opponent.

The imaginary line that divides the table lengthwise is called the long string, and the rails on the long sides of the table are called the long rails. Each player is allowed to use only one half of the table and his ball must stay within the confines of his half of the table without touching the long rail. If a player's ball crosses the long string, touches the long rail, or otherwise leaves his half of the table, he loses the lag. If the balls collide near the long string, and it cannot be determined that one of them crossed the center line, the players should lag again.

Fouls

Any of the following occurrences constitutes a foul:

- a scratch—the cue ball is pocketed
- shooting the cue ball off the table
- shooting while balls are moving or spinning
- failing to pocket a ball, or failing to cause a ball to contact a cushion
- striking the cue ball twice on the same shot
- unless the cue ball is in hand, touching it with the hand or clothing

Spotting Balls

The term *spotting a ball* refers to placing a ball on the foot spot. This is required in some games, when a ball is pocketed on a shot where a foul is committed. If a ball cannot be placed on the foot spot without interfering with other balls, it is placed as close as possible to the foot spot on a line between the foot spot and the center diamond on the foot rail.

14.1 CONTINUOUS OR STRAIGHT POOL

Object of the Game

Each ball counts as 1 point. A game of straight pool is played to a predetermined number of points, usually 100 or 150. The first player to reach that number of points wins.

Opening Rack

All 15 numbered balls are racked at the normal foot spot position. Balls can be in any position in the rack.

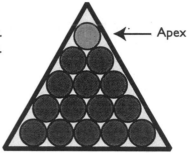

Straight pool rack for the initial break.
All balls are placed at random.

Apex

Subsequent Racks

Balls may be shot from the opening rack until only one object ball remains on the table. That last remaining object ball becomes the break ball for the following rack. Both the cue ball and the break ball are left in place; only the remaining 14 balls are included in the rack, with the apex spot left vacant.

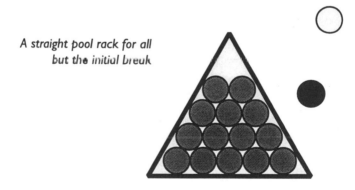

A straight pool rack for all
but the initial break

If any part of the last remaining object ball interferes with racking the balls, it is included in the rack at the apex position.

If any part of the cue ball interferes with racking the balls, the shooter has it in hand behind the head string.

The Opening Break

For a legal opening break, the shooter must call a ball and pocket, or shoot a safety.

A safety on the break requires that two object balls and the cue ball strike a cushion after initial contact.

Failure to meet one of these two criteria is a foul and results in a 2-point penalty, which may result in a negative score. And the opponent has the option of accepting the table or having the balls reracked and rebroken by the original shooter.

A scratch on an otherwise legal break is a 1-point penalty.

Play

The shooter can shoot at any ball in any order so long as he calls the ball to be pocketed. In calling a ball, he must indicate which ball and in which pocket. A ball pocketed, but not called, is spotted by returning it to the table on the foot spot or as close to the foot spot as other balls may allow.

The shooter need not hit the called ball first, nor does he have to describe intervening balls, cushions, and so on.

A legal shot is any shot in which the player pockets a called ball, causes the object ball to be driven to a cushion, or causes the cue ball to be driven to a cushion after hitting an object ball.

Fouls are a 1-point penalty. Three consecutive fouls is an additional 15-point penalty.

When only 1 object ball remains on the table, the remaining 14 balls are racked with the apex ball position vacant. The player who made the last ball continues to shoot until he misses. He may attempt to pocket the break ball and break the balls in the rack, or play a legal safety.

A player may play a safety. A legal safety is a shot that

causes the object ball to be driven to a cushion, or causes the cue ball to be driven to a cushion after hitting an object ball.

9-BALL

The game of 9-ball has become the championship game of U.S. pocket billiards. It has displaced straight pool in tournament play and is now the game most widely played by professional players.

The Object of the Game

The object of 9-ball is to pocket the 9-ball, either on the break or on any other legal shot.

Nine-ball is a rotation game in that, on each shot, the cue ball must strike the lowest-numbered ball first. Otherwise it is a foul.

The Rack

Only the balls numbered 1 through 9 are used; they are racked in a diamond shape. There are special diamond-shaped racks made for 9-ball, but it is more common to use a triangle rack and leave the spaces for three balls at each lower corner vacant. The 1-ball is always placed on the foot spot at the apex of the triangle, and the 9-ball must be the center ball. Other numbered balls may occupy any position.

The 9-ball rack. The gray balls are numbers 2 through 8 and are placed at random.

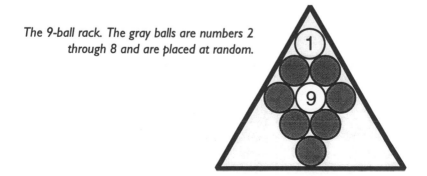

The Break

For the opening break, the player may place the cue ball anywhere behind the head string. The 1-ball, being the lowest-numbered ball on the table, must be struck first when breaking.

Also, for a legal break, at least four numbered balls must be driven to a rail.

All balls pocketed on the break, except the cue ball and the 9-ball, remain pocketed. If the 9-ball is pocketed on the break and the shooter scratches, the 9-ball is spotted.

A foul on the break gives control of the table to the other player, with cue ball in hand.

Play

The cue ball must strike the lowest-numbered ball first, and as long as that happens, any other balls pocketed count.

If the 9-ball is pocketed on any legal shot, the shooter wins.

As on the break, if the shooter fouls, all balls remain pocketed except the 9-ball, which must be spotted.

If the shooter fouls while shooting the 9-ball, he loses.

Fouls on three consecutive shots results in a loss if your opponent has warned you after the second foul that he plans to invoke the rule.

Push Out

The player at the table immediately after a break has the right to call a push out. This allows the shooter to shoot the cue ball to any other place on the table without contacting any other ball or rail. The shooter must announce to his opponent that he is shooting a push out; otherwise it is considered a normal shot. The only way to foul on a push out is to pocket the cue ball.

After a push out, the incoming player may either accept the table and continue with normal play, or refuse the table, in which case the other player resumes normal play.

8-BALL

The most popular game in the United States is 8-ball.

Object of the Game

The object of 8-ball is to pocket all of your assigned group of balls (either stripes or solids), and then pocket the 8-ball.

The Rack

The game of 8-ball is played with a full rack of 15 balls and begins with the apex ball of the rack on the foot spot. Within the rack, the 8-ball must be the center ball. One solid ball and one striped ball must each occupy a lower corner position.

The 8-ball rack

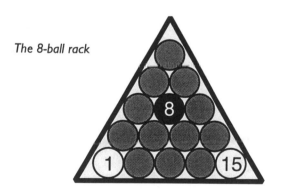

The solid and the stripe in the corners can be reversed and may be of any number within their respective groups.

The Break

For the opening break, the player may place the cue ball anywhere behind the head string. The cue ball does not have to contact the apex ball for a legal break, but the player must either pocket a ball or drive at least four balls to a rail.

If the 8-ball is pocketed on the break, the shooter can either request a rerack and break again, or spot the 8-ball and continue shooting.

The first player to pocket a ball after the break (balls pocketed on a break are ignored) is assigned the balls of that group, either stripes or solids. His opponent is automatically assigned the other group. For example, if I break and pocket the 2-, 5-, and 11-balls, I get to shoot again because I pocketed a ball; which balls I pocketed are immaterial. If I then miss my shot, it is your turn. If you make the 15-ball, you are assigned stripes and I am assigned solids. Play now resumes, with our shots limited to the balls in our respective groups.

How to Win the Game

A game is won when a player, having pocketed all of his group of balls, pockets the 8-ball on a subsequent shot.

How to Lose the Game

The game is lost by a player who:

• pockets the 8-ball out of turn.
• fouls or scratches while shooting at the 8-ball.
• pockets the 8-ball in other than the called pocket.
• pockets the 8-ball and final object ball on the same shot.

House Rules

There are as many sets of house rules for 8-ball as there are places to play. It is possible that more money has been lost, and more fights started, because of house rules for 8-ball than any other game.

Needless to say, if you're going to play 8-ball, be sure you understand the house rules in the establishment where you're playing. And as an added precaution, ask to see them and read them for yourself—don't rely on the interpretation of others, especially not your opponent.

ONE-POCKET
The idea behind one-pocket is that each player has only one corner pocket into which he may pocket balls that count. It is a game of skill, defense, and strategy.

The Break
All 15 numbered balls are racked on the foot spot. The numbers have no value, so balls can be positioned at random. For the opening break, the player has the cue ball in hand behind the head string.

Play
Before the break, each player chooses one of the corner pockets at the foot of the table.

The first player to make eight balls in his pocket wins.

Balls pocketed in either corner pocket count for the person who owns the pocket.

Balls pocketed in the four unused pockets are spotted after the shooter misses or when no balls remain on the table.

ROTATION
Rotation, in many areas of the country, is called slop pool, because it lends itself to shooting as hard as possible and hoping that something goes in.

The Break
All 15 balls are racked on the foot spot with the 1-ball at the apex and the 2-ball and 3-ball at the other corners. Remaining balls can be placed at random.

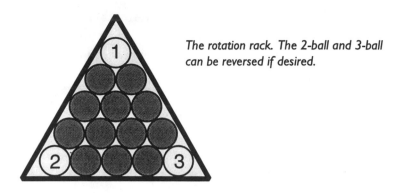

The rotation rack. The 2-ball and 3-ball can be reversed if desired.

The shooter must hit the 1-ball for any other pocketed balls to count; otherwise any pocketed balls are spotted.

On the break, the shooter has the cue ball in hand behind the head string.

Play

On each shot, the shooter must hit the lowest-numbered ball first; after this, any pocketed ball counts as the number value on the ball.

The number values of the 15 balls total 120. Consequently, the first player to reach 61 points wins the game.

If a player makes a legal shot, pockets a ball, but causes other balls to jump off the table, the jumped ball is respotted; it is not a foul. Under any other circumstances, a ball leaving the table ends the inning.

CUTTHROAT

The game of cutthroat is designed for three players. As determined by the lag for break, the player who breaks is assigned balls 1 through 5, the runner-up on the lag is assigned balls 6 through 10, and the remaining player is assigned balls 11 through 15. The last player to have balls on the table wins.

The Break

Players lag for break. All 15 balls are racked on the foot spot. The 1-ball should occupy the apex position, and the 6-ball and 11-ball are placed in the other corners.

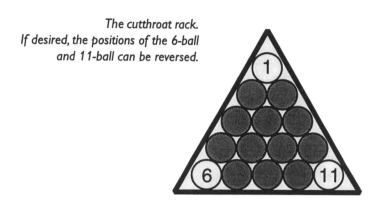

The cutthroat rack.
If desired, the positions of the 6-ball
and 11-ball can be reversed.

The shooter to break has the cue ball in hand behind the head string.

Play

Balls may be shot in any order and in any pocket.

A player may pocket his own balls or his opponents' balls and, in doing so, remains at the table.

In the event of an illegal shot, any opponent's ball pocketed is spotted, but if the shooter's own ball(s) is pocketed, it remains down. If the shooter scratches or jumps the cue ball from the table, he is penalized by having one ball for each opponent returned to the foot spot.

If a player has no balls on the table when it is his turn, he is eliminated without a shot, and the table is turned over to the following player.

Subsequent Games

For the next game, the loser of the previous game becomes the breaker and is assigned balls 1 through 5; the runner-up of the previous game shoots second and is assigned balls 6 through 10; the winner of the previous game shoots last and is assigned balls 11 through 15.

GLOSSARY

Action - A game for money; as in "Let's go in and see if there's any action."

Balance point - The point on the cue, normally about 16 inches from the butt, where the cue will balance on a finger or fulcrum.

Ball in hand - Being able to place the cue ball anywhere on the table for your next shot.

Bank shot - Any shot in which the object ball strikes a cushion before being pocketed.

BCA - *See* Billiard Congress of America.

Bed - The playable surface of a table, usually made of slate.

Billiard Congress of America - The official governing body of pocket billiards played or sanctioned in the United States.

Billiards - Any of the group of games played on a rectangular table with cushions (with or without pockets).

Billiard table - A rectangular table with cushions bounding the playing area, but without pockets. *See also* Pool table.

Break - The first shot of any game.

Bridge - Use of the front hand to control the shaft of the cue.

Bumper - The rubber knob on the bottom of the cue that protects it when it's rested on the floor.

Butt - The large end of a cue stick. Although the term *butt* is often used to mean the entire lower half of the cue, it actually only refers to the portion of the cue below the wrap (the area where the cue is gripped).

Call shot - A rule that requires the shooter to specify the ball to be pocketed, and the pocket into which it will be made, prior to making the shot.

Center string - An imaginary line that passes between the centers of the side pockets.

Chalk - A caked powder in a small cube that is applied to the cue tip to create friction between the cue tip and the cue ball.

Cheat the pocket - Shooting the object ball to the left or right side of the pocket in order to create an angle for position play. This is commonly done on a shot that would otherwise be straight in.

Combination - A shot in which the cue ball first contacts a ball other than the one to be pocketed.

Cripple - An object ball right in front of a pocket that cannot be missed.

Crutch - Slang for a mechanical bridge.

Cue - The stick used for shooting pocket billiards.

Cue ball - The white (unnumbered) ball used to shoot at object (numbered) balls.

Cue ball in hand - *See* Ball in hand.

Cuing - Using other than a center hit to control the movement of the cue ball.

Cushion - The raised, cloth-covered rubber bumper that surrounds the playing area of a table.

Cut shot - Any shot in which the cue ball contacts the object ball off center and thus drives the object ball in a direction other than the cue ball's original path.

Cutthroat - One of many games played in pool. *See* "Cutthroat" in chapter 8.

Dead-ball shot - *See* Stop shot.

Dead stroke - Similar to playing on autopilot; a player is at peak level, and playing without conscious effort or thought.

Diamonds - The dots along the rails that divide them into even increments.

Dots - *See* Diamonds.

Draw - A method of cue-ball control that causes the cue ball to move back toward its point of origin after contacting the object ball.

Drop pockets - A pool table with no gully system, so balls remain in the pockets where they were made.

Double elimination - A tournament format in which players are not eliminated until they lose two matches.

8-ball - One of many games played in pool. *See* "8-Ball" in chapter 8.

English - A method of cue-ball control that puts spin on the cue ball.

Feather shot - An extremely thin cut shot in which the cue ball just barely grazes or touches the object ball.

Ferrule - A piece of protective material (normally white) between the shaft and the cue tip.

Flat draw - A low hit on the cue ball (but not as low as normal draw); it's often used to change the cue ball's angle of deflection off the object ball.

Follow - A method of cue-ball control that causes the cue ball to move forward after contacting the object ball.

Follow-through - The action of stroking "through" the cue ball after the tip contacts the ball.

Foot spot - The spot marked on the foot of the table where the balls are racked. It is centered on the table, 2 diamonds from the foot rail.

Foot string - An imaginary line that passes between the second diamonds on the long rails and through the foot spot.

Force draw - Applying very powerful draw on the cue ball, thereby causing the maximum amount of draw.

Force follow - Applying very powerful follow on the cue ball, thereby causing the maximum amount of follow.

Forearm - On two-piece cues, the area of the cue between the joint and the wrap.

Foul - A rules violation that causes a player to lose his turn at the table.

14.1 continuous - One of many games played in pool. *See* "14.1 Continuous or Straight Pool" in chapter 8.

Frame - A player's turn at the table, also known as an inning.

Frozen - When a ball is in firm contact with a cushion or another ball.

Grip - Holding the cue with your rear hand.

Gully - On a pool table, a rail under the pockets that returns all pocketed balls to a common box at the foot of the table.

Handicap - A scoring method that evens the chances among players of varying skill levels.

Head spot - The spot marked on the head of the table that is in the center of the table and 2 diamonds from the head rail.

Head string – An imaginary line that passes between the second diamonds on the long rails and through the head spot.

Hustler – A player who takes advantage of less skillful participants in money games. The ethics of such players are dubious.

Inning – A player's turn at the table.

Jaw – The part of the cushion that is cut to form the opening of the pocket.

Joint – The two fittings that are screwed together to connect a two-piece cue.

Jump shot – Intentionally causing the cue ball to become airborne so that it jumps over balls obstructing its path to the object ball.

Jump the table – Accidentally causing the cue ball or any object ball to leave the table. It is normally a foul.

Kick – Causing the cue ball to contact one or more cushions before striking the object ball.

Kill shot – *See* Stop shot.

Kiss – Two ball that are touching.

Lag – Determining who will break. Each player shoots a solid ball (not the cue ball) from behind the head string to the foot of the table. The player whose ball returns closest to the head rail wins the lag and the break. The winner of the lag may elect to pass the break to his opponent.

Leave – The arrangement of the balls after a shot.

Long string – An imaginary line that runs from the center of the head rail to the center of the foot rail.

Masse shot – A shot with extreme English, which is applied by holding the cue at a position of 30 to 90 degrees while applying left or right spin.

Mechanical bridge – A notched metal or plastic plate attached to the end of a stick that is used as a bridge in situations where the use of a hand bridge is impossible.

Miscue – When the cue strikes the cue ball improperly and slides off.

Natural English – English applied to the cue ball that accentuates the direction the cue ball would have traveled naturally.

9-ball – One of many games played in pool. *See* "9-Ball" in chapter 8.

Object ball – Any numbered ball that you're shooting at or that is the next ball to be pocketed.

One-pocket – One of many games played in pool. *See* "One-Pocket" in chapter 8.

Pool table – A rectangular table with cushions bounding the playing area and six pockets. Regulation size is 4½ feet x 9 feet.

Position play – Consistently controlling the movement of the cue ball after it strikes the object ball to gain a subsequent favorable shooting position.

Push out - In 9-ball, the first player to shoot following the break can elect a push out, which is a kind of free shot. Pocketing the cue ball and causing the cue ball to leave the table are the only fouls. Any balls pocketed are spotted. The incoming player may make a legal shot or hand the table back to the player who pushed out.

Race - The number of games needed to win a match—for instance, a race to 7.

Rack - The triangular wood or plastic device used to position the balls for the start of the game.

Rake - Slang for a mechanical bridge.

Rotation - One of many games played in pool. *See* "Rotation" in chapter 8.

Run - The series of balls pocketed in one inning.

Run out - A series of balls pocketed in one inning to win the game.

Safety - A defensive move designed to leave your opponent without a shot.

Scratch - Pocketing the cue ball.

Set - *See* Race.

Shaft - The narrow, tapered end of a cue stick to which the tip is attached.

Sharking - Any one of numerous acts that unethical players employ to rattle or upset their opponent.

Shooting system - A term embraced by the BCA to indicate all of the fundamental components that go into making a shot—stance, grip, bridge, stroke, and so on.

Shot - The action that begins when the cue tip contacts the cue ball and ends when all balls have stopped moving.

Single elimination - A tournament format in which a player is eliminated after the loss of a single match.

Snookered - When the object ball lies behind another ball and cannot be struck by the cue with a direct hit.

Stance - The way a player stands at the table in the shooting position.

Stick - *See* Cue.

Stop shot - A shot in which the cue ball stops immediately upon impact with the object ball.

Straight pool - *See* 14.1 continuous.

Table - *See* Pool table.

Tip - The end of the cue stick that strikes the cue ball. Normally the tip is made of leather or a composition material.

Triangle – *See* Rack.

Wrap – The part of the cue, near the butt, designed for the player's grip.

A VERY SHORT READING LIST

The following book offers excellent reading for the player who wishes advanced information to supplement this work: *99 Critical Shots in Pool,* by Ray Martin. This is a useful reference for many of the shots you'll frequently encounter and the various ways you can approach them.

INDEX

Martin, Ray, 7, 42
Mechanical bridge, 19
Mental game, 12
   See also Brain, training the
Miscue, 76
Mizerak, Steve, 7, 16
Mosconi, Willie, 7, 16, 67, 69

9-ball pool, 60, 63, 66, 84
   rules, 97-99

Object ball, 12
   focus on, 25
   stroke practice, 45
One-pocket pool, 101

Pattern play, 42, 62-64
Planning ahead, 65-66
Players, average, 13-14
Pocket billiards, 9, 62
Pocketing balls, 12
Pool, objectives of, 9-10
Pool table, 11
   See also Tables
Position play, 31, 64, 66-67, 69
Powder, 83, 86
Power break, 60, 84
Practice strokes, 21
Push out, 98-99

Rear hand, 14
Record, written, 23
   See also Checklist, pre-pool